Mary Mulari's
Garments with Style

Adding Flair to Tops, Jackets, Vests,
Dresses, and More!

Other Books Available from Chilton

Robbie Fanning, Series Editor

Contemporary Quilting

Appliqué the Ann Boyce Way

Barbara Johannah's Crystal Piecing

The Complete Book of Machine Quilting, Second Edition, by Robbie and Tony Fanning

Contemporary Quilting Techniques, by Pat Cairns

Fast Patch, by Anita Hallock

Fourteen Easy Baby Quilts, by Margaret Dittman

Machine-Quilted Jackets, Vests, and Coats, by Nancy Moore

Pictorial Quilts, by Carolyn Vosburg Hall

Precision Pieced Quilts Using the Foundation Method, by Jane Hall and Dixie Haywood

Quick-Quilted Home Decor with Your Bernina, by Jackie Dodson

Quick-Quilted Home Decor with Your Sewing Machine, by Jackie Dodson

The Quilter's Guide to Rotary Cutting, by Donna Poster

Quilts by the Slice, by Beckie Olson

Scrap Quilts Using Fast Patch, by Anita Hallock

Speed-Cut Quilts, by Donna Poster

Stitch 'n' Quilt, by Kathleen Eaton

Super Simple Quilts, by Kathleen Eaton

Teach Yourself Machine Piecing and Quilting, by Debra Wagner

Three-Dimensional Appliqué, by Jodie Davis

Three-Dimensional Pieced Quilts, by Jodie Davis

Craft Kaleidoscope

Creating and Crafting Dolls, by Eloise Piper and Mary Dilligan

Fabric Painting Made Easy, by Nancy Ward

How to Make Cloth Books for Children, by Anne Pellowski

Jane Asher's Costume Book

Quick and Easy Ways with Ribbon, by Ceci Johnson

Learn Bearmaking, by Judi Maddigan

Shirley Botsford's Daddy's Ties

Soft Toys for Babies, by Judi Maddigan

Stamping Made Easy, by Nancy Ward

Too Hot To Handle? Potholders and How to Make Them, by Doris L. Hoover

Creative Machine Arts

ABCs of Serging, by Tammy Young and Lori Bottom

The Button Lover's Book, by Marilyn Green

Claire Shaeffer's Fabric Sewing Guide

The Complete Book of Machine Embroidery, by Robbie and Tony Fanning

Craft an Elegant Wedding, by Naomi Baker and Tammy Young

Creative Nurseries Illustrated, by Debra Terry and Juli Plooster

Distinctive Serger Gifts and Crafts, by Naomi Baker and Tammy Young

The Fabric Lover's Scrapbook, by Margaret Dittman

Friendship Quilts by Hand and Machine, by Carolyn Vosburg Hall

Gail Brown's All-New Instant Interiors

Gifts Galore, by Jane Warnick and Jackie Dodson

Hold It! How to Sew Bags, Totes, Duffels, Pouches, and More, by Nancy Restuccia

How to Make Soft Jewelry, by Jackie Dodson

Innovative Serging, by Gail Brown and Tammy Young

Innovative Sewing, by Gail Brown and Tammy Young

The New Creative Serging Illustrated, by Pati Palmer, Gail Brown, and Sue Green

Owner's Guide to Sewing Machines, Sergers, and Knitting Machines, by Gale Grigg Hazen

Petite Pizzazz, by Barb Griffin

Putting on the Glitz, by Sandra L. Hatch and Ann Boyce

Quick Napkin Creations, by Gail Brown

Second Stitches: Recycle as You Sew, by Susan Parker

Serge a Simple Project, by Tammy Young and Naomi Baker

Serge Something Super for Your Kids, by Cindy Cummins

Sew Any Patch Pocket, by Claire Shaeffer

Sew Any Set-In Pocket, by Claire Shaeffer

Sew Sensational Gifts, by Naomi Baker and Tammy Young

Sew, Serge, Press, by Jan Saunders

Sewing and Collecting Vintage Fashions, by Eileen MacIntosh

Simply Serge Any Fabric, by Naomi Baker and Tammy Young

Singer Instructions for Art Embroidery and Lace Work

Soft Gardens: Make Flowers with Your Sewing Machine, by Yvonne Perez-Collins

The Stretch & Sew Guide to Sewing on Knits, by Ann Person

Twenty Easy Machine-Made Rugs, by Jackie Dodson

Know Your Sewing Machine Series, by Jackie Dodson

Know Your Bernina, second edition

Know Your Brother, with Jane Warnick

Know Your Elna, with Carol Ahles

Know Your New Home, with Judi Cull and Vicki Lyn Hastings

Know Your Pfaff, with Audrey Griese

Know Your Sewing Machine

Know Your Singer

Know Your Viking, with Jan Saunders

Know Your White, with Jan Saunders

Know Your Serger Series, by Tammy Young and Naomi Baker

Know Your baby lock

Know Your Pfaff Hobbylock

Know Your Serger

Know Your White Superlock

Star Wear

Embellishments, by Linda Fry Kenzle

Jan Saunders' Wardrobe Quick-Fixes

Make It Your Own, by Lori Bottom and Ronda Chaney

Shirley Adams' Belt Bazaar

Sweatshirts with Style, by Mary Mulari

Teach Yourself to Sew Better, by Jan Saunders

A Step-by-Step Guide to Your Bernina

A Step-by-Step Guide to Your New Home

A Step-by-Step Guide to Your Sewing Machine

A Step-by-Step Guide to Your Viking

Mary Mulari's Garments With Style

Adding Flair to Tops, Jackets, Vests, Dresses, and More!

Chilton Book Company

Radnor, Pennsylvania

Copyright © 1995 by Mary Mulari

All Rights Reserved

Published in Radnor, Pennsylvania 19089, by Chilton Book Company

Designed by Rosalyn Carson
Color photography by G.W. Tucker Photographic Studio
Black-and-White photography by Margaret Croswell
Illustrations by the author

On the front cover: Four garments start out plain and get style. Shown clockwise from top are: the Tuxedo Shirt with Pillow Panel from Section 25; stepping rectangles on a pink vest (a variation of the Man's Shirt with Stepping Rectangles found in Section 30); the Southwest-Style Denim Jacket from Section 33; and the Vest with Ultrasuede Squares and Yam Couching from Section 19. Front cover photographs by Donna H. Chiarelli.

On the back cover: Strips of colorful VIP fabrics convert a man's shirt into a lightweight jacket with style, Josephine's Coat of Many Colors (Section 29), and woven fabric strips and fringe add same-color trim to an aqua blazer (see Section 34). Back cover photographs by G.W. Tucker Photographic Studio.

Manufactured in the United States of America

Library of Congress Cataloging-in-Publication Data

Mulari, Mary.
    (Garments with style)
    Mary Mulari's garments with style: adding flair to tops, jackets, vests, dresses, and more!
        p.   cm.—(StarWear)
    Includes bibliographical references (p. 142) and index.
    ISBN 0-8019-8640-0 (pbk.)
    1. Clothing and dress—Decoration. 2. Clothing and dress—Alteration. 3. Machine applique. I. Title. II. Title: Garments with style. III. Series.
TT552.M85 1995
746.9'2—dc20   94-23783
                                                      CIP

1 2 3 4 5 6 7 8 9 0   4 3 2 1 0 9 8 7 6 5

The following registered trademark terms appear in this book:
Aleene's Hot Stitch Fusible Web
Dritz Magic Fuse
Dylon
Fasturn
Fiber Etch
Fiskars
Fray Check
Heat-Away
HeatnBond Lite
Husqvarna Braiding Guide
Lycra
Magic Sizing
Miraclestitcher
Pearls 'N Piping Foot
Perfect Sew
Post-it Notes
Rinsaway
Scotchlite
Sliver
Solvy
Pellon Stitch-N-Tear
Stitch Witchery Plus
Teflon
Totally Stable Iron On Stabilizer
TransWeb
Ultrasuede
Velcro
Wonder-Under
Woolly Nylon

Are you interested in a quarterly newsletter about creative uses of the sewing machine and serger, edited by Robbie Fanning? Write to *The Creative Machine*, P.O. Box 2634-B, Menlo Park, CA 94026.

This book is dedicated, with appreciation, to my father, Arvid J. Koski. His continued interest, support, and entrepreneurial motivation have encouraged me in my business and in life.

Contents

Foreword

For years, Mary Mulari has been traveling all over the country teaching from her popular books. That's how we first met. I hired her to teach at my sewing shop in Clinton, Iowa, and the customers loved her and bought her books like crazy. The second time I invited her, I billed her as the "Applique Goddess." The crowd was not disappointed. Mary's seminars, like her books, are full of great ideas, designs, and concise, complete instructions.

It was Mary who introduced me to "Stitch-N-Tear," and she also helped me discover the beauty of applique with Ultrasuede. So you can imagine how honored I was to preview this, her latest book.

In *Garments with Style*, Mary takes decorating "blank" garments to new heights. With each chapter, she encourages us to experiment with a new sewing technique, and along the way we redesign our plain clothes into something unique and original.

And this is a book that is just right for our life and times. Our days are moving at warp speed. Our daily pace is so hectic, we almost feel guilty if we take time out of our schedule to sew. How can we expand our sewing skills if we never devote any time to this hobby we love?

Enter...*Garments with Style*. Mary tempts us into using "twisting serger strips" on the front of a plain dress. Wow! We have a new outfit that suits our personal style and is completed in just a few hours.

See what I mean? You don't have to worry about feeling like a failure because it will be years before you complete the heirloom quilt you began long ago. Instead, take the plain suit jacket out of the closet and experiment with a woven shoulder cover or Battenberg lace around the lapels.

This book has changed my shopping habits. I can hardly wait to visit my local consignment shop for some likely candidates for a style makeover. (What I really need is a navy blue man's suit vest for the "Quick Change Vest.")

Thanks again, Mary. This book will be a valuable addition to anyone's sewing library. Once again, you've managed to introduce me to new and exciting ideas. You never fail to amaze me, Girl!

Rita Farro
Sewing author, teacher, and orignator of "How To Dress With Style When You Feel Like Cher But Look Like Roseanne" seminars

Acknowledgments

My name is on the cover of this book as the author, but a strong cast of supporting companies and individuals deserves my thanks and recognition. Like the winners at any awards ceremony, I have names to list because they have made an important contribution to this book.

Sincere thanks to Alpha Shirt Company, Bagworks, Bernina of America, C. J. Enterprises, Concord Fabrics, Creative Crystal Company, Elna Inc., Fiskars, Handler Textile Corporation, Max e.b., New Home Janome Sewing Machine Company, C.M. Offray & Sons, P & B Textiles, Palmer/Pletsch, Pfaff American Sales Corporation, Prym Dritz, Signature Threads, Sulky of America, Sunbelt, Therm O Web, Viking Sewing Machine Company, VIP Fabrics, and Wimpole Street Creations.

To the people who listen to me, share their ideas and honest opinions, and offer encouragement, I am also grateful. Their suggestions and assistance with this book are invaluable. Special thanks to Gail Brown, Rita Farro, Donna Fenske, Nancy Harp, Sarah L. Koski, Barry Mulari, Nancy Ward, Nancy Zieman, and to my niece, Sarah Faith Koski, for modeling garments. And to my everyday support group, the Sunset Acres A.M. Walking Women, thanks for your perspective and good humor.

For this, my second book for Chilton Book Company, I appreciate again the assistance and valued contributions of my editor, Susan Keller, and Series Editor Robbie Fanning.

And thanks to you, my readers, who have bought, read, and used my books for many years and responded so positively to what you have found in them. More times than you know, you've inspired me and made my day.

Bright Idea

Look for hints and other helpful information in these "Bright Idea" boxes scattered throughout the book.

Introduction 1

For many years I have decorated sweatshirts. They were the first kind of "blank" garment for which I, and probably you, saw great possibilities. Sweatshirts are easy to buy or make; they are comfortable to wear; and, with our personalized touches, they have become even more interesting. But, in concentrating on sweatshirts, we have overlooked many other kinds of plain clothes: shirts, vests, jackets, sweaters, T-shirts, and more. So with this book I have had a great time exploring the potential of an expanded wardrobe, and I hope you too will enjoy trimming a wider range of garments.

Think of all the possibilities. Are there clothes that have been pushed to the back of your closet and considered lost causes? Are there garments you've made or bought that could use just a touch of trim or updating? You can even buy clothing at a consignment shop with a specific trimming project in mind. By adding style to a garment, you transform it into something more attractive and something you're more likely to wear. And, in most cases, you'll be recycling your clothing as you improve it.

If you have the urge to sew and would like to trim plain clothes, this book can help with the challenge of turning something ordinary into something extraordinary. We'll start off with the basics of where to find garments to trim, what supplies and equipment to have on hand, and how to machine applique and make patterns from sections of whole garments. Please read these sections carefully, because they contain information you'll need to know to be able to create your own garments with style. After these basics come 34 sections containing over 40 projects, many with full-size applique designs and all with plenty of inspiration to help you create truly personalized clothing.

I've organized the projects in this book by garment. All the vests are in one section, the jackets in another, and so on. It is important to remember, though, that a trim idea that I've shown on one kind of garment—a jacket, for example—can usually be applied to many other kinds of garments. Don't hesitate to look beyond the project in the book to see other possibilities. Perhaps the trim could be used in a different location on the garment; perhaps different colors or materials could be used. My notes in the "Bright Ideas" boxes might give you additional insights. By adding your personal touch to my ideas and suggestions, you'll be creating your own works of art. The chapter on designer labels will show you how to add your signature to your sewing and serging creations.

Make this book your own by adding notes in the margins. If you'd like the book to lie open and flat while you're using it, take the book to a print shop and ask for a spiral binding to replace the present binding. I encourage you to do anything that makes the book easier to use.

As you try the projects in the book and develop your own ideas, you are welcome to write to me and share your thoughts. It's always great to know how you've interpreted my words and suggestions in the projects you've completed. My address is Box 87-C2, Aurora, MN 55705.

Let's get started! All your plain clothes are calling for help.

Selecting Garments & Supplies
Part One

Plain Clothes & Where to Find Them

2

Plain clothes are easy to find. You can buy them, make them, and find them hiding in the back of your closet or dresser drawer. Once you've added your designer touch to these clothes, they are no longer ordinary and you'll be wearing them more often.

Consignment stores are another source for plain clothes. These stores resell clothing provided to them by individuals. People bring in clothes that they are tired of or that no longer fit them in the hope that the store will be able to sell the garments. Both the store and the seller get a portion of the sale price. Consignment stores also sometimes offer new clothing left over from factory orders or discounted from regular retail shops.

Before deciding to trim a garment, consider its fit and condition. A garment that fits well and that was sewn or purchased specifically for trimming is a good candidate for the projects in this book. It makes sense to spend time decorating a worthy garment: one that fits comfortably, is made of quality fabric, and is in good condition.

But what about the garments hanging in the closet, rejected and unworn? Sometimes we keep clothing for sentimental or other unexplainable reasons, and these pieces

could be eligible for sewing transformation projects. If you have a T-shirt that fits and you still like the color, but you have nothing to wear with it, consider trimming the shirt in colors to coordinate with a skirt you like to wear. Once again, however, the criteria of fit and condition should be applied. If the shirt shows any signs of wear, a pilled surface, or fading, it's not worth your valuable time and sewing skills to revive it.

Is there a stain on a special garment? If the garment fits and is in good condition, you may be able to cover the stain with an applique. But the stain must be in a location that is suitable for decorating. When you try on the garment to make sure that it fits, figure out just where an applique covering the stain would be positioned. Because clothing will change in dimension when it is put on a human body, the only way to see how a decoration will look when a garment is worn is to try on the garment. By trying on the garment and planning the location of your designs *before* you sew, you'll avoid many sewing disasters.

My recommendation for any clothing you decorate is that it be in new or nearly new condition. This applies equally to garments that are hiding in your closet and that you find in consignment stores.

This is like warning knitters not to knit with cheap, poor-quality yarn. You will regret using good materials, your talent, and precious sewing hours on a garment that will look aged after one or two launderings.

And speaking of laundering, I also suggest that you consider the washability of a decorated garment. If you want to be able to wash the T-shirt, dress, or jacket the same way you did when it was plain, make sure to add to it fabrics and trims that are also washable.

One place to find plain clothing to decorate is in your closet. With the ideas in this book, you'll be able to give a new life to ordinary garments. Then, instead of hanging in the closet, those forgotten clothes will be worn and appreciated again.

Consignment Shopping Interview with Jolly & Linda

3

As I was preparing the manuscript for this book, I thought it would be a great idea to interview two consignment shopping experts. Readers who have never considered this way to purchase clothing might be encouraged to check out a consignment shop after you read Jolly Michel's and Linda Funk's thoughts about their favorite way to shop. Jolly Michel is the Dean of Agribusiness and Consumer Services at Southwest Wisconsin Technical College in Fennimore, and Linda Funk is the Director of National Product Communications for the Wisconsin Milk Marketing Board in Madison. Both are home economists, have traveled extensively, and have checked out consignment stores in many locations.

Here is our interview and the ideas they shared with me.

MM:

Why is consignment shopping a good idea? How do you get past the stigma that it's a "low-class" activity?

JM & LF:

You can do very well consignment shopping if you know clothing labels and the cost of buying the same quality at retail. You can have a larger wardrobe for less money. We think it's a great way to economize on clothing. Though we don't see consignment store shopping as low class, we believe that you do need to shop with the right attitude. We see consignment shopping as a sport, and finding a piece of clothing that's just right is the thrill of the hunt. Frequently, you'll find high-quality clothing at consignment stores—you'll be very pleasantly surprised.

We'd recommend shopping for the first time with someone who is experienced with consignment stores. You might even shop out of town if you don't want to be seen. When you visit a good consignment store and discover what's there, you'll realize the potential of this new shopping adventure.

MM:

What do you look for as good features in a consignment store?

JM & LF:

Many of the stores where we like to shop have attractive window displays, which is a good first clue about the store. We also like stores that have displays within the store, that are well organized, and that have no musty odor when you walk in the door.

MM:

Do you take anything along when you shop, besides an open mind and money?

JM & LF:

We suggest a sense of humor first of all. If we have a garment we're trying to match up with something, we take it along. A tape measure is often handy to have for quick measurements of clothing. We also suggest a pair of foam shoulder pads, as sometimes they're gone from the garments we try on. A pair of dress heels is convenient to have along, if you're shopping for or find something dressy.

MM:

What are the benefits of shopping with friends? Tell me about your consignment shopping rules.

JM & LF:

Friends who can be honest with you and also enjoy the sport are the best kind to take along. We often make our shopping day a special occasion by meeting for breakfast and planning the day. We have a list of shops we want to visit, along with a map, if that's needed. Anyone who has a special item of clothing on her wish list describes what she's looking for. We also plan for several breaks during the day, as all this fun shopping can be tiring.

The rules we have are that everyone has to buy something, or at the least try something on. We shop for everyone in the group, and we ignore the sizes on garments. Many times, they've been labeled wrong, and that's why they're in the shop in the first place. Either that, or the sizing is very different from what you might expect. To be a good consignment shopper, you can't be married to your size. It's another instance of how it helps to be open-minded. You can always cut out the size tag if it bothers you after you buy it.

MM:

How do you inspect clothing? What flaws make you lose interest in a garment? What kinds of problems on clothing can be fixed easily?

JM & LF:

First of all we look for the style and color of the clothing. If that appeals, then it's a good idea to inspect the garment inside and out. We check to see that the garment isn't badly soiled or stained under the arms, problems which would discourage us from buying it.

Because we sew, we don't see hems or ripped seams or linings to be problems we can't fix. Changing buttons is easy and can really improve most clothing. Missing shoulder pads can be replaced, and if sleeves aren't long enough for you, they can be turned into short sleeves.

MM:

What about pills on clothing?

JM & LF:

Those ugly little bumps on fabric might discourage us too, but we've found that electric clothes shavers have helped eliminate that problem on some clothes.

MM:

Worn areas on the shoulders are a sign that something has been hanging around a long time. Do you see shoulder areas as a problem?

JM & LF:

We do see garments with problems on the shoulders, sometimes from light exposure and there are faded lines where the hanger is. This might be an area that can be covered and embellished, and we think you might have some ideas for that, Mary. (Yes, I do; see Sections 25, 27, and 34, for example.)

MM:

How do you determine if the consignment store price on a garment is good or fair?

JM & LF:

It helps to know quality in ready-to-wear and in fabric. If you sew, you know fabric costs and the time it takes to make a quality outfit. Sewing expertise is helpful to consignment shopping, because you can purchase a fine garment and adjust the fit, if necessary. You don't have to hire someone to do that for you. We enjoy remaking something more than sewing it from scratch.

MM:

What is a real find at a consignment store?

JM & LF:

We're always excited to find designer labels, high-quality fabrics, and garments we know we could never afford at ready-to-wear prices. Specialty fabrics like silk and wool gabardine are especially attractive to us.

Men's blazer jackets are often a find at a terrific price. They're usually made of better fabrics than what's available in women's clothing, and they can be restyled to fit women, especially women with slim figures. Try them on to see what you think. We think that a blazer with no open back vents looks a bit more feminine. (For instructions, see *Innovative Sewing*, by Gail Brown and Tammy Young.)

Then there was the Christian Dior wool coat at a New York City consignment store. It was in perfect condition, and the price was $125; the silk suit in Dubuque, Iowa, was only $35; the Ultrasuede suit in Chicago was $40. . . . We could go on and on.

MM:

How do you handle consignment clothing once you've purchased and brought it home? Do you dry-clean or wash everything first?

JM & LF:

If the items are washable, we do that. We think that people who sew have a good sense about what fabrics can be laundered, and they'll take the time to wash something carefully. If dry cleaning is required, that may prevent us from buying the garment since that adds significantly to the price, depending on what the garment is.

MM:

How are consignment stores different from thrift shops?

JM & LF:

Thrift stores are generally run by a charity group, and we find that the quality of merchandise and the prices are generally lower than consignment stores. It's possible to find treasures at thrift stores, but we recommend that you try consignment stores first as they can be more pleasant in terms of shopping atmosphere.

MM:

Any advice for consignment shoppers?

JM & LF:

Ask your friends if they can recommend any good stores. You might be surprised at how many people have discovered the joys of consignment shopping. Check the yellow pages of the phone book. You might get hooked on this activity and even search out stores while you're on vacation in another city. We have enjoyed many hours of searching for trophy finds in consignment stores, and we hope you'll try it too.

Bright Idea

To help rejuvenate a not-so-new garment that you're considering for a sewing transformation, spray on Magic Sizing before pressing to firm up and smooth the fabric.

Sewing Supplies, Materials, & Equipment 4

*E*ach project in this book begins with a list of supplies and the type of garment to use. Fabric and yardage estimates are intended to be generous so you will not run out of the materials you'll need to complete the project. It is always a good idea to read through the entire set of instructions before beginning to sew; that way there will be no surprises in the process.

General sewing-room supplies will be part of most projects. Your sewing machine, the iron, and ironing board should all be ready to use. (I dream of the day my ironing board will be perfectly clear of sewing stuff and I will be able to iron the legs of a tall person's pair of pants without doing it in 12" sections!) (Fig. 4-1).

Figure 4-1: A typical view of my overloaded ironing board

Pins, scissors, measuring tools (yardstick, ruler, and tape measure), and a rotary cutter, ruler, and cutting mat are also important tools for most garment transformations.

Here are other supplies I recommend that you have available.

Stabilizers

There are many varieties of stabilizers. So many of the fabrics we sew on need the extra firmness of a stabilizer, which is placed on the wrong side and removed after the stitching is completed.

Tear-away stabilizers are literally torn away from the back of the stitching areas. Water-soluble stabilizers can also be torn away, but they have the added advantage of dissolving in water and do not have to be ripped from the fabric. The advantage of an iron-on stabilizer is that it is pressed on the back of fabric and pins are not needed to hold it in place. Newer, iron-away stabilizers are made of a muslin type of fabric that is burned away by the heat of the iron and brushed off the fabric with an old toothbrush. Liquid and spray-on stabilizers are also available and, when applied to fabric, stiffen the treated areas so that stitching can be accomplished without puckering or distorting the fabric.

I suggest that you experiment with many types of stabilizers and find what works best for you and the fabrics you sew on. Investigate the varieties at a fabric store. Stabilizers are especially helpful when sewing decorative stitching or appliques onto knits and onto many of the ready-made garments you'll use for this book's projects. Here are some brand names of stabilizers, listed by type: tear-away—Stitch-N-Tear Pellon; water-soluble—Solvy and Rinsaway; iron-on—Totally Stable Iron On Stabilizer; vanishing muslin—Heat-Away; and liquid—Perfect Sew.

Paper-Backed Fusible Web

Paper-backed fusible web has revolutionized applique; fusing it to the wrong side of the applique fabric and then cutting out a design guarantees that the applique's edges will be firmly attached to the base fabric and that the design will lie smooth and flat against the base fabric. It can also be a big time saver when used to fuse hems or edges of fabric in place. Many brands and varieties of this product are available. Make sure to use a weight appropriate for sewing; some of the heavier weights of paper-backed fusible webs are not recommended for sewing through. Brand names include HeatnBond Lite, Wonder-Under, Dritz Magic Fuse, TransWeb, Stitch Witchery Plus, and Aleene's Hot Stitch Fusible Web. Fusible web is available in two forms: on a bolt and in narrow rolls; both are convenient to use (Fig. 4-2).

Figure 4-2: Paper-backed fusible web is sold by the yard from a bolt or in narrow rolls.

Ultrasuede

You will notice that I chose Ultrasuede for the decorations in many of the projects in this book. It has wonderful advantages: It won't fray, ravel, or shrink; it looks elegant; and it's machine washable and dryable. If the high price of Ultrasuede has kept you from trying it, consider using scraps and small pieces to help you overcome your fear of working with the fabric. I'm convinced that once you work with Ultrasuede, you will want to do many more projects with this suede-like fabric. Mail-order sources of Ultrasuede pieces and scraps are listed at the back of the book.

Tricot Knit Interfacing

Tricot knit interfacing is a lightweight, soft variety of interfacing that has a fusible backing. It gives a sufficient amount of stability and body to most fabrics used in this book's projects.

Tissue Paper

Tissue paper—yes, the kind you buy for gift wrap—is just right for making the garment patterns needed for this book's projects. It also serves well as an ironing board protector when fusing lace. It's one of the things piled high on the end of my ironing board.

Tracing Paper

Tracing paper comes in tablet form and is available at office-supply or stationery stores. The paper is very sheer and easier to see through than tissue paper. For some projects, it's important to be able to trace designs from fabric. Having a tablet of this translucent but sturdy paper around will be a help to you.

Clear Nylon Thread

Clear nylon thread makes it easy to have nearly invisible stitches. Generally, it is used only as the top thread on garments (the bobbin thread is standard sewing thread, which is softer against the skin). Depending on your stitch choice, nylon thread can nearly disappear into the applique fabric or the garment. Available in both a clear and a darker tone, this thread is a good basic to keep on hand (it's 0.004mm thick).

Specialty Scissors

Pinking shears provide an easy way to trim and clip seam allowances all at the same time; they leave a neat zigzag edge on nonfray fabric. Pelican-billed applique scissors are handy for trimming away fabric close to the seam line and are valued for their sharp tips, which can cut very precise corners and edges (Fig. 4-3).

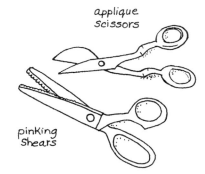

Figure 4-3: You'll appreciate having these special scissors for many of the projects in this book.

Fray Check

Just a drop of this liquid prevents raveling on serged seams, ends of ribbon, and other raw edges.

Jeans Needle

When sewing on denim, as we'll do for some of the projects in this book, using a jeans needle on the sewing machine is a smart idea. This needle maneuvers through denim more smoothly than regular needles, which might easily break in thick denim seams. Jeans needles are now available in a variety of sizes.

Press Cloth

A piece of protective fabric—a press cloth—will be used many times as we fuse Ultrasuede to garments and for other pressing also. Always keep it handy at the ironing board.

Using and experimenting with new sewing products can prove to be a smart way to sew and to increase your sewing skills. Even if you learned to sew without tools like rotary cutters, applique scissors, and stabilizers, you're wise to adapt to new equipment and materials—sewing's bound to become more efficient for you, and more fun too.

General Instructions Part Two

The Basics of Machine Applique

5

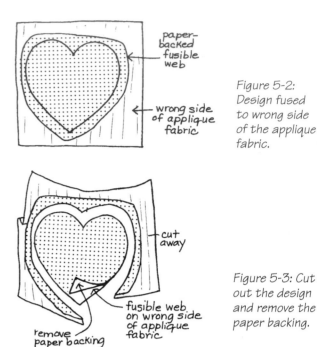

Figure 5-2: Design fused to wrong side of the applique fabric.

Figure 5-3: Cut out the design and remove the paper backing.

Since many of the trim projects and techniques in this book are based on applique, I'll begin with basic instructions for machine applique. More detailed directions are available in other books (see the Bibliography), including my book *Sweatshirts with Style*.

Sewing machine applique, often called satin stitching, is a skill that improves with practice, so don't be embarrassed if your first efforts look less than perfect.

Trace an applique shape onto the paper side of paper-backed fusible web and cut the paper slightly larger all around than the design shape. If the design has an obvious right and left side, trace the mirror image of the original design (Fig. 5-1).

Place the design (right side of fabric up) on the right side of another piece of fabric on which you will sew the design. Fuse in place, following the manufacturer's directions. Place a piece of stabilizer larger than the design shape on the wrong side of the base fabric (Fig. 5-4). After this preparation, you're ready to sew.

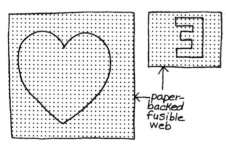

Figure 5-1: Trace designs on the paper side of paper-backed fusible web. Remember to reverse any designs with a definite right and left side, such as the letter E.

Following the manufacturer's instructions and suggestions for iron temperature, fuse the design to the wrong side of the applique fabric (Fig. 5-2). Cut out the design along the lines you traced and peel off the paper. Now the design shape has a smooth backing, like an iron-on patch (Fig. 5-3).

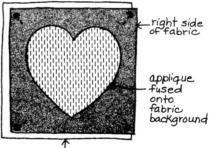

Figure 5-4: Remember to add a stabilizer to the fabric before sewing.

Use the sewing machine applique stitch to attach a floral design to a plain shirt front.

Begin with a new sewing machine needle (size 80/12 or 90/14) and first-quality, new thread. (Walk quickly past the barrels advertising 10 spools for $1.00. This kind of thread is not worthy of your sewing abilities.) Attach an open toe or applique presser foot to your machine; check the machine's instruction manual to help you select a correct presser foot (Fig. 5-5).

Figure 5-5: The correct presser foot, such as this open-toe foot, will make it easier to guide the applique stitching.

Adjust the sewing machine to a zigzag stitch with a short stitch length (Fig. 5-6).

← zigzag stitch

← zigzag with short stitch length is satin stitching

Figure 5-6: Shorten the length of the zigzag stitch to get the applique or satin stitch you want for traditional machine applique.

Note that on some machines you will have to loosen the sewing machine's top tension for a more attractive applique stitch. Practice by sewing a variety of lines of applique stitches on stabilized fabric (Fig 5-7).

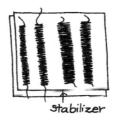

stabilizer

Figure 5-7: Experiment with different widths of applique stitches.

Adjust the stitch width to see what setting looks best to you. Make notes about which machine adjustments produce the stitching you like best. When you're ready to sew around your applique design, begin stitching in the center of a line, not a corner. Guide the stabilized fabrics so the needle sews over the design edges (Fig. 5-8). After stitching around the entire shape, overlap a few stitches, pull the threads to the back of the fabric and knot. Remove the stabilizer.

Figure 5-8: Cover the edge of the applique design with applique stitches.

This basic method of machine applique can be used for all the applique designs in this book. I've provided a flower shape to help you practice (Fig. 5-9). To explore other applique options, try one of the methods used in the following projects:

- Invisible applique: T-Shirt with Attached Vest (Section 11)

- Dimensional applique: T-Shirt Front Yokes with Fringe or Lace (Section 12)

- Reverse applique: T-Shirt Hood with Reverse Applique (Section 13)

- Overlay applique: Overlay Applique Tunic (Section 14)

- Decorative stitch applique: Man's Shirt with Stepping Rectangles (Section 30)

- Lined applique: Sweater with Lined Argyle Applique (Section 36)

- Puckered applique: Sunflower Apron (Section 40)

Bright Idea

Ultrasuede is a friendly applique fabric in many ways. It's machine washable and dryable, it won't ravel, it fuses in place (with a press cloth over it to protect its surface), and the colors are luxurious. A beginning sewer can straight stitch the shapes in place; satin stitching skills aren't required. Work with small pieces until you get comfortable with it. Once you start using it, it'll be hard to stop!

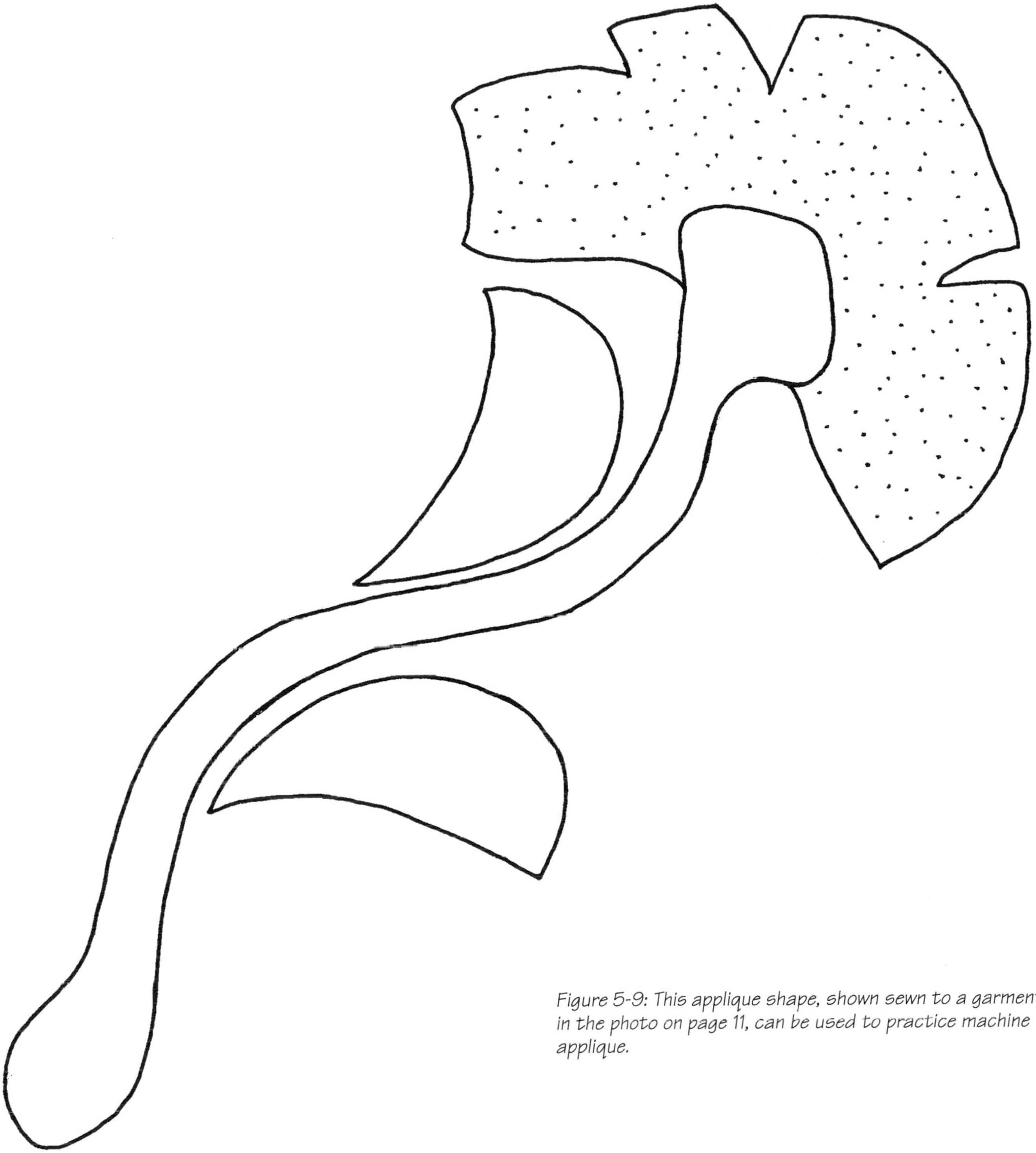

Figure 5-9: This applique shape, shown sewn to a garment in the photo on page 11, can be used to practice machine applique.

Making Patterns from Garments by Pin Tracing

6

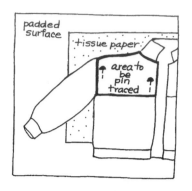

Figure 6-1: Layer tissue paper and the portion of the garment to be pin traced on a padded surface.

Y ou'll use this easy pattern-making technique for several transformations that require covering a portion of a garment with another piece of fabric. Don't let the title scare you away; professional sewing experience is not required for this method of capturing a pattern from a section of a garment.

SUPPLY LIST

GARMENT TO BE DECORATED

TISSUE WRAPPING PAPER

PINS

NEEDLE OR T-PIN FOR POKING THROUGH THE GARMENT

PADDED SURFACE TO WORK ON

CHALK MARKER OR WATER-SOLUBLE MARKING PEN

1 First, set up a padded working surface for this project. It could be a surface of corrugated cardboard, two layers of towels, or a bed. If you prepare a padded surface on a tabletop, make sure the table is well protected from the pins that will be pushed through the garment, tissue, and padded layers. I'd never forgive myself if you messed up your walnut dining room table.

2 On the padded surface, place a sheet of tissue paper large enough to cover the garment area you plan to trace. Over the tissue, lay out the portion of the garment, making sure it is flat. To anchor the garment to the tissue and padded surface, pin the layers together in the center of the garment, away from the edges of the area to be traced (Fig. 6-1).

3 Decide whether a pin or needle will be used to make the marks in the tissue. If the garment is a fine delicate fabric such as silk, use a needle. If the fabric is thicker, use a T-pin. Push the needle or pin through the garment into the tissue paper along the outer edge of the area to be traced. Do this all the way around the pattern area, at approximately ½″ (1.3cm) intervals. Make sure to mark the points where lines intersect (Fig. 6-2).

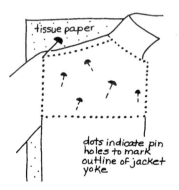

Figure 6-2: Push a pin through the garment to mark the lines of the section you want to trace.

Check the pin marks in the tissue paper before removing the entire garment and the anchoring pins. If you can't see the pin holes, make larger ones or more of them in the tissue paper. Then remove the garment and anchor pins. Mark the grain line of the garment fabric on the tissue paper (Fig. 6-3).

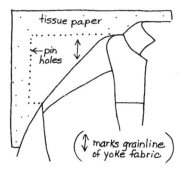

Figure 6-3: Make sure you can see the pinhole markings in the tissue paper.

4 Draw a line to connect the pin holes on the tissue paper (Fig. 6-4). Cut out the pattern, the actual shape of the garment section, from the tissue by cutting on the lines you drew. Seam allowances are added when you cut the pattern from fabric.

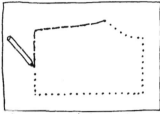

Connect pin hole markings to draw outline of pattern.

Figure 6-4: Draw a line connecting all the pinholes to form the pattern.

5 Place the pattern piece on the chosen fabric, allowing ⅝" (1.5cm) or more around all the edges of the pattern. Make sure the grain line drawn on the pattern is in line with the grain of the fabric. Using a chalk marker or a water-soluble marker, trace the pattern piece on the fabric. Cut out the pattern, adding the seam allowance (Fig. 6-5).

line marking actual size of pattern copied from garment

⅝" seam allowance

Figure 6-5: Add a ⅝" (1.5cm) seam allowance to all sides of the actual pattern shape.

6 Place the fabric piece over the garment and pin in the center. Turn under and pin the seam allowances. Be sure that the folded edges of the fabric (the actual pattern line drawn on the fabric) line up with the edges of the garment area (Fig. 6-6).

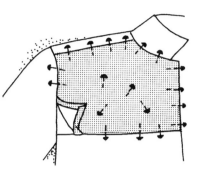

Figure 6-6: New fabric cover pinned in place over the jacket.

If the seam allowances are too bulky or wide, trim them away. For areas such as necklines and sleeve seams that curve, clip into the seam allowance so that the fabric will lie flat and more easily line up with the garment's seams (Fig. 6-7).

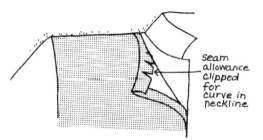

Seam allowance clipped for curve in neckline

Figure 6-7: The neckline seam allowance is clipped to help fit the fabric to the garment.

7 After you have finished pinning, topstitch around the edges of the new fabric to cover the garment..

See, it wasn't so difficult. Once you've tried this method, you'll find it easy to pin-trace parts of any garment.

*T-Shirts,
Tunics, &
Tank Tops
Part Three*

T-Shirt with Print Cutouts for Applique

7

Using sections of printed fabric is a great way to produce appliques for a garment. I like to look for prints with shapes that have smooth and easy edges to cut around, like the one I used on the purple T-shirt in the photo on page 18. Of course, you could straighten out the edges of many shapes, such as flowers with jagged edges. Remember, you're the artist and you can reshape and design as you wish.

To imitate ready-to-wear, try sewing a coordinating garment from the same print fabric you used to decorate the top. Consider making a skirt, shorts, or a jacket. You may prefer to sew the garment first and then use the scrap fabrics for trimming a shirt.

SUPPLY LIST

1 PLAIN T-SHIRT

PRINTED FABRIC (AMOUNT VARIES DEPENDING ON PRINT, APPLIQUE DESIGN, AND COORDINATING GARMENTS MADE)

1/4 YD. (23CM) PAPER-BACKED FUSIBLE WEB

1/2 YD. (46CM) TEAR-AWAY STABILIZER (OPTIONAL)

1 1/2 YD. (1.38M) SOUTACHE OR OTHER NARROW BRAID (OPTIONAL)

1 Select the print shapes you want to use for applique. On the wrong side of the fabric, fuse slightly larger pieces of paper-backed fusible web to the shapes. Cut the shapes from the fabric and peel off the paper backing; now you're ready to arrange the shapes on the garment.

2 It may be easier to plan the design arrangement while wearing the shirt. Try the shirt on and carefully pin the applique shapes to the garment. I am always inclined to encircle the shirt neckline, forming a yoke that frames the neck and face. It's usually a flattering formation, and you might want to try it (Fig. 7-1).

Figure 7-1: Fabric shapes arranged to circle the neckline of a T-shirt.

3 Fuse the shapes to the shirt. After fusing, place a stabilizer on the wrong side of the garment and stitch the shapes to the shirt. I used a machine blanket stitch (Fig. 7-2) and red thread on the garment in the photo, but a standard satin stitch would work well to cover the fabric's raw edges. Other stitches could also be used. You might practice and experiment on scraps before you begin stitching on the shirt.

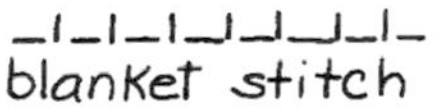

_|_|_|_J_J_J_|_
blanket stitch

Figure 7-2: The blanket stitch is a popular alternative applique stitch.

4 An additional element added to the shirt is a curving line of narrow soutache braid sewn over the applique shapes—a bit of passementerie-style trim. The braid is optional, but it helps to unify the design because it touches on each of the separate applique pieces (Fig. 7-3).

Figure 7-3: A curving line of narrow braid adds another dimension to the shirt's appliques.

5 Use the curve shown in Figure 7-3, or draw your own to accent the appliques on your T-shirt. It is easier to guide the trim around gentle curves than sharp corners. Draw the line with a chalk marker or a water-soluble pen.

6 Note that the trim starts at the right shoulder, where it is inserted into the shoulder seam of the shirt. It's easy to open up a tiny portion of the seam, insert the trim end, and restitch the shoulder seam. This detail suggests that the design could have been added to the shirt front before the shirt was assembled, a detail you see on ready-to-wear garments.

7 Select thread to match the color of the braid; use a presser foot that has an opening in front leading directly to the needle. This opening will accommodate braid or cord. Use a bit of gluestick on the wrong side of the braid to help keep it in place on the line of your design while you're sewing it to the shirt. Sew over the braid with a straight stitch or a narrow zigzag to attach the braid to the shirt.

8 The use of stabilizer on the underside of the shirt is optional and may depend on both the type of braid used and the stability of the T-shirt fabric. You might try sewing on the braid without a stabilizer; check after 1″ (2.5cm) of sewing and add stabilizer if the braid or the fabric is rippling.

T-Shirt with Print Cutouts for Applique

Cut design shapes from printed fabric to trim a plain T-shirt. Add a curving line of narrow braid trim over the top of the designs to introduce another dimension to the shirt's trim. A pair of shorts made from the same print fabric creates a unique outfit.

9 The end of the soutache braid flows over the left shoulder to the back of the T-shirt, and zigzag stitching holds it in place (Fig. 7-4).

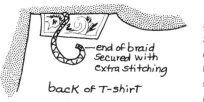

Figure 7-4: Secure the end of the braid with zigzag stitching and backstitching.

Challenge yourself by studying some of the printed fabrics in your current stash or on bolts of material at the fabric shop. You'll soon notice the possibilities for applique shapes.

Mixed Media T-Shirts

8

*U*sing the size and shape of a Battenberg doily as the guide for other fabrics, I decorated the T-shirt shown on page 20 with a variety of fiber media: lace, painted fabric, buttons, yarn, ribbon roses, and Ultrasuede strips. It's fun to study a few decades' worth of accumulated sewing supplies for inspiration. I'll bet you have a great supply of collectibles that could be showcased on a T-shirt front.

T-Shirt with Lace & Painted Fabric

SUPPLY LIST

1 PLAIN T-SHIRT

FABRIC PAINT (OPTIONAL)

1 SPONGE OR FOAM RUBBER BRUSH (OPTIONAL)

ONE 5″ (12.5CM) SQUARE OF CORRUGATED CARDBOARD (OPTIONAL)

SCRAPS OF FABRIC AND LACE

ONE 3 1/2″ (9CM) SQUARE BATTENBERG DOILY

TISSUE WRAPPING PAPER

1/4 YD. (23CM) PAPER-BACKED FUSIBLE WEB

1/4 YD. (23CM) STABILIZER

ASSORTED RIBBONS, BUTTONS, AND YARN FOR TRIM

1 The square in the center of the blue T-shirt shown in the photo is white fabric—painted with corrugated cardboard! If you'd like to try this unique fabric enhancement, assemble your supplies—fabric paint, 5″ (12.5cm) squares of corrugated cardboard, and a sponge or foam rubber brush—and cover your working surface. I prefer to do this in my "project room" (sometimes called a kitchen) near the sink. Run warm water over the edges of the corrugated cardboard pieces, and you will find it easy to remove one of the flat surfaces, revealing the ribbed section in the center (Fig. 8-1). Let the cardboard dry before painting with it.

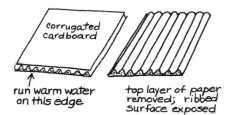

Figure 8-1: Corrugated cardboard before and after the top layer is removed.

2 With a sponge or foam rubber brush, wipe fabric paint over the ribs of the corrugated surface. Press the cardboard square onto the fabric and carefully remove the cardboard. Brush more paint onto the ribs and turn the cardboard so you'll produce a gridded design when you press it down on the fabric again (Fig. 8-2). Wait until the paint dries, and then heat-seal the paint with an iron, following the manufacturer's instructions. Now you can cut a design from the painted fabric. Who would ever guess you created the design with a simple piece of cardboard?

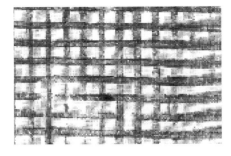

Figure 8-2: This design formed by pressing the paint-covered ribbed surface of corrugated cardboard onto fabric.

Mixed Media T-Shirts

Use a variety of trims and accents to create mixed media T-shirts. Squares of lace, printed fabrics, a doily, and painted fabric encircle the neckline of the blue T-shirt (from Alpha Shirt Company), with a mixture of buttons and ribbons sprinkled on top of everything. Fringed pieces of denim enhanced with decorative stitching and fabric swatches trim the mauve T-shirt.

3 Trace the Battenberg doily, or another shape, onto paper-backed fusible web to make five designs. Fuse the web patterns to the wrong sides of the chosen fabrics. Be sure to use white tissue paper under the Battenberg doily (and lace, if you're using it) when you fuse the paper-backed web. That way, the extra fusing material will stick to the tissue, not your ironing board or iron. Discard the used tissue paper. After fusing the web, cut out the shapes and remove the paper backing.

4 Arrange the shapes on the shirt. I chose a semicircular design around the neckline. If you want, continue the designs to the back of the shirt. To test your design, pin the shapes to the shirt and try it on. When you are satisfied with the design layout, fuse the shapes onto the T-shirt.

5 Place stabilizer on the wrong side of the shirt before sewing the appliques. As seen on ready-to-wear garments, I used a medium-width zigzag stitch and matched the thread color to the shirt. The stitching detail shows up more on some of the fabric squares than others. It's faster to sew when you don't have to change thread colors (Fig. 8-3).

Figure 8-3: Zigzag stitching secures the edges of each fabric applique.

6 After you have finished sewing the appliques onto the T-shirt, plan the extra trims you want to add. I enjoyed searching through my button collection, ribbon box, and yarn basket when I trimmed the blue T-shirt. Shank buttons and ribbon roses can be attached with safety pins pinned from the wrong side of the shirt if you want to remove them before laundering. Sew-through buttons can be sewn on in the normal (boring?) way or with yarn, which makes a more prominent attachment (Fig. 8-4).

Figure 8-4: A variety of ways to sew buttons on with yarn.

Another method for attaching this style of button is to sew pieces of ribbon to the garment and then thread the ribbon through the holes in the buttons; tie the ribbons into a bow or knot to hold the button in place (Fig. 8-5). Have fun trying a variety of methods when you attach buttons to your T-shirt.

Figure 8-5: Sew the center of a ribbon to the shirt and use it to tie on a button.

T-Shirt with Fringed & Decorated Denim

The mauve mixed media T-shirt in the photo features a different selection of decorating ideas from the blue shirt (see above). You might mix and match the ideas from these two shirts to come up with a unique garment all your own. The patches of denim on the mauve shirt were frayed and decorated with stitching before they were attached to the shirt front. Lines of decorative stitching connect the patches.

SUPPLY LIST

1 PLAIN T-SHIRT

SMALL SCRAPS OF DENIM FABRIC FROM OLD JEANS

1/4 YD. (23CM) PAPER-BACKED FUSIBLE WEB

SMALL SCRAPS OF FABRIC FOR DECORATING THE DENIM PIECES

1/4 YD. (23CM) TEAR-AWAY STABILIZER (OPTIONAL)

LIQUID STABILIZER

1 Cut and fray the denim patches before decorating them. Who says that the edges of frayed patches have to be cut straight? You'll notice that some of the patches on this shirt have wavy and uneven edges, which adds a bit of extra interest. Some of the patches were cut with a Fiskars wavy-edge rotary cutter (Fig. 8-6).

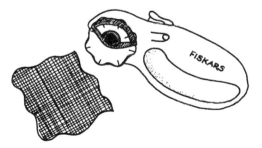

Figure 8-6: Use a wavy-edge rotary cutter to add extra interest to the patches for this project.

Because the patches for this project are not large (Fig. 8-7), it won't take long to fringe their edges. Look at both sides of your denim patches; you may want to use the wrong side of some patches as the right side for this project.

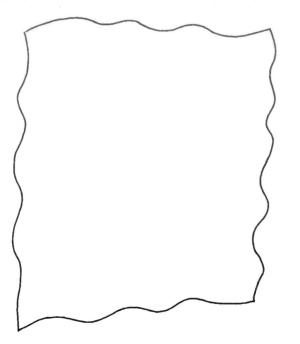

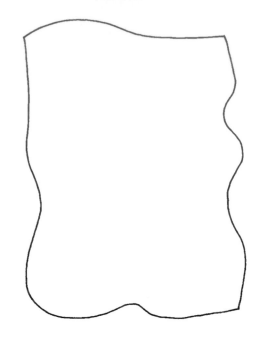

Figure 8-7: Applique shapes for the denim patches.

2 Cut pieces of paper-backed fusible web for the wrong side of each fringed patch; the web should cover only the center unfrayed portion of the fabric and not the fringe. Fuse the web in place on each patch and leave the paper on the fabric.

3 Add stitching to the right side of the patches. I recommend using satin variety stitches for the patches, as they stand out well on denim. I used several colors of rayon threads when I stitched the patches for my T-shirt. I also fused small pieces of decorative fabrics on the denim and then stitched around these smaller patches (Fig. 8-8). The paper of the fusible web will help to stabilize the denim fabric while you sew around the smaller patches. When the stitching is done, tear away the paper from the back of the web; don't worry about the small pieces of paper that remain in the stitching. Now the patches are ready to be fused to the T-shirt.

Figure 8-8: Small pieces of fabric and decorative stitches in rayon threads adorn the denim patches.

4 Plan the locations of the patches after marking the bustline on the shirt (to avoid placing the decoration where it will look awkward). Fuse the shapes to the shirt and then sew them to the shirt, stitching along the inside edge of the

fringe. I used navy thread and a narrow zigzag stitch. I did not need to use a stabilizer when sewing on the patches, but a flimsier T-shirt might require it.

5 Using a chalk marker, draw stitching lines on the shirt to connect the patches. These lines will be sewn with decorative stitching. Wet the lines you've drawn on the shirt with a liquid stabilizer, such as Perfect Sew (Fig. 8-9). Once the shirt is dry, you'll be ready to sew the lines with your choice of decorative stitching. The stabilizer prevents the stitching from sinking into the knit fabric; instead, the stitching will lie flat and all the details of the decorative stitch will be visible. After the shirt is complete, rinse the garment to remove the stiffened stabilizer from the stitching lines.

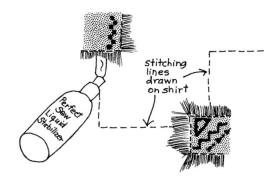

stitching lines drawn on shirt

Figure 8-9: Wet the stitching lines with liquid stabilizer; allow the shirt to dry before sewing the decorative stitches.

Combine the ideas from the two shirts presented here to create your own mixed media clothing.

Stars & Stripes T-Shirt 9

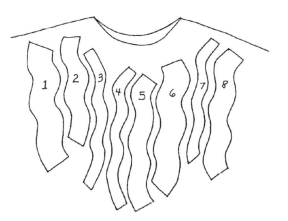

Figure 9-1: Numbered stripes in position on the front of the T-shirt.

*I*nstead of traditional straight-line stripes, this T-shirt features wavy stripes of different widths, with stars sprinkled over them and silver streamers attached to the stars. For the shirt shown on page 24, I used tricot-backed lamé for the stripes, Lycra for the stars, and heavy silver thread (normally used for serging) for the streamers.

SUPPLY LIST

1 PLAIN T-SHIRT

PAPER FOR MAKING TEMPLATES

1/2 YD. (46CM) PAPER-BACKED FUSIBLE WEB

1/2 YD. (46CM) FABRIC FOR STRIPES

1/2 YD. (46CM) TEAR-AWAY STABILIZER

ASSORTED FABRICS FOR STARS

4 YD. (3.6M) OF HEAVY THREAD FOR STAR STREAMERS

1 Trace the three stripes from page 26 onto paper and cut them out. Make two paper shapes of the widest stripe and three *each* of the two narrower stripes. The paper templates will help you plan the design on the T-shirt.

2 Following the photo and Figure 9-1, arrange and pin the paper stripes on the front of the T-shirt. Try the shirt on to check the arrangement. Number the paper stripes, beginning on the left side of the shirt, to indicate the stripe positions as well as the right side of the stripe. Before unpinning the paper stripes, trace them or portions of them, onto the shirt with a water-soluble marker; the traced lines will serve as guidelines for placement of the fabric stripes.

3 When tracing the paper stripes onto the paper-backed fusible web, remember to flip them over so that the numbered side of the stripe is against the paper layer. This will guarantee that the design will turn out as you planned. Write the number of the stripe on the paper-backed fusible web (Fig. 9-2).

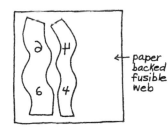

Figure 9-2: Trace the paper stripes in reverse on paper-backed fusible web.

4 Fuse the web stripes to the wrong side of the fabric you've selected for the stripes. Cut them out; remove the paper backing; and with help from the numbers, place them in order on the shirt. Fuse them in place. After placing stabilizer on the wrong side of the shirt beneath the stripe area, sew the edges of the stripes. I used clear nylon top thread and bobbin thread to match the shirt. I attached the stripes with a narrow blind hem stitch (Fig. 9-3).

Stars and Stripes T-Shirt and Doily Yoke T-Shirt

Choose special fabrics to add interest to T-shirt decorations. Tricot-backed silver lamé fabric and colorful Lycra fabrics are the choices for the stars and stripes on the navy shirt (Section 9). Strands of heavy silver threads are inserted beneath the stars for shiny streamers. Added to the neckline of the red sleeveless T-shirt (Section 10) is a purchased doily and a drawstring casing made from the original neck ribbing of the T-shirt.

--^--^--^-- blind hem
stitch

Figure 9-3: The blind hem stitch sewn with clear nylon thread creates a nearly invisible stitching line.

5 Now you're ready to plan the star locations on top of the stripes. Trace five star patterns onto paper (using the pattern on p. 26) and cut them out. Position and pin the paper templates on the shirt, as you did with the stripes. Use the shirt in the photo as a model or create your own arrangement. Try on the shirt to make sure the stars are not placed directly on the bustline. Trace the stars onto the shirt with a water-soluble marker and unpin the paper templates.

6 Using the paper templates, trace five stars onto paper-backed fusible web. Fuse the web to the wrong side of the star fabrics, and cut out the stars.

7 Add streamers to the bottom edge of the stars before fusing the stars to the shirt. An easy way to make the streamers is to wrap the thread around four fingers eight times. Hold the top of the threads in place over your index finger and cut the streamers in half below your little finger (Fig. 9-4).

cut fringe here

Figure 9-4: Make streamers for the stars by winding thread around your fingers.

Place the center of the folded streamers beneath the lower edge of the star; fuse the star to the shirt; and then sew around the edges, securing the streamers to the shirt at the same time (Fig. 9-5). Repeat for the other stars.

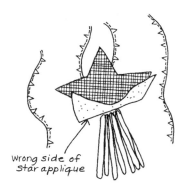

wrong side of star applique

Figure 9-5: Place the thread streamers beneath the edge of the star before fusing the applique to the T-shirt.

This design idea can be interpreted in red, white, and blue—to represent the flag—or any other color combination.

Bright Idea

A package of construction paper in assorted colors has helped me to design appliques and choose colors. Invest in a package of your own for your sewing room. It might also help to keep young children busy if they keep you company when you sew.

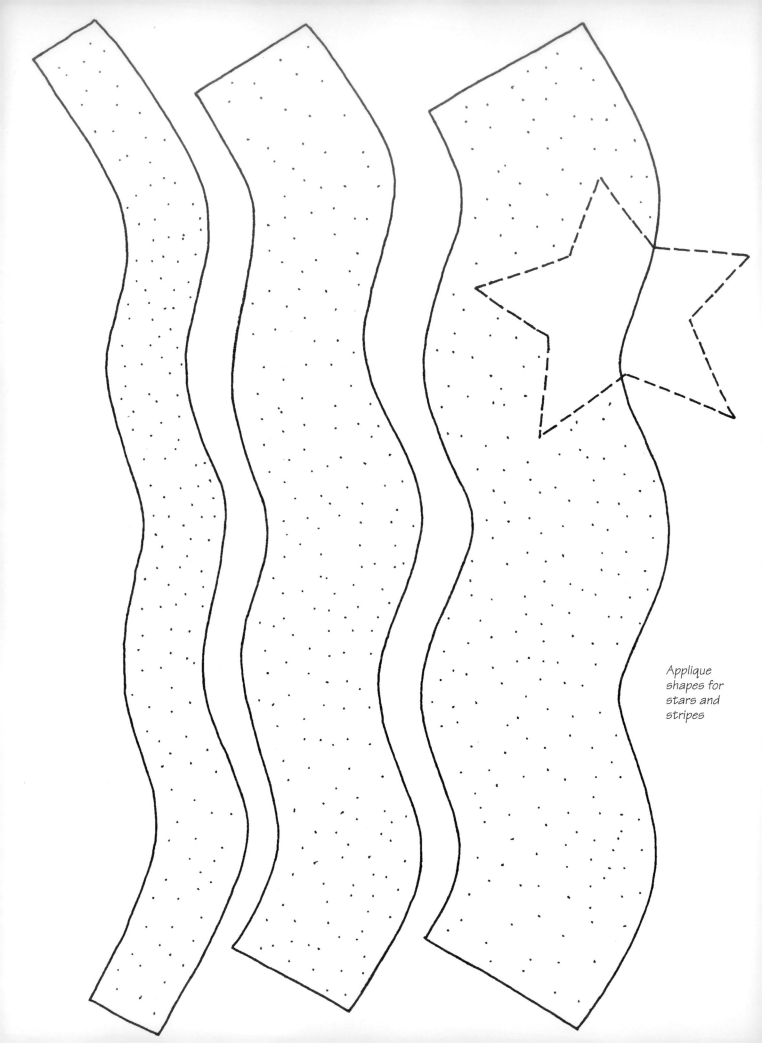

Applique
shapes for
stars and
stripes

Doily Yoke T-Shirt 10

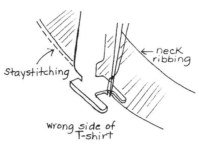

A purchased doily, or one from your grandmother's collection, adds a touch of style to a plain T-shirt neckline. The doily encircles the face, serving as a flattering frame. The new neckline is a portion of the neck ribbing that has been made into a casing; a ribbon is laced through it (Fig. 10-1).

SUPPLY LIST

1 PLAIN T-SHIRT WITH NECK RIBBING

1 DOILY, 15" (38CM) IN DIAMETER, OR LARGER

NARROW BIAS TAPE (1/2" [1.3CM] OR NARROWER) TO COVER INSIDE BACK NECK SEAM (OPTIONAL)

1 YD. (91.5CM) NARROW RIBBON OR CORD FOR DRAWSTRING

1 Removing the neck ribbing is the first step in this project. Stabilize the neck edge of the T-shirt by staystitching around the neck before cutting off the neck ribbing. To do this, straight stitch on the wrong side of the T-shirt very close to the stitching that attaches the neck ribbing. If you can adjust the position of your sewing machine needle, move the needle to the right. (Fig. 10-2).

2 Carefully cut away the ribbing. Remember that you'll be using it again to make the drawstring casing, which is sewn at the neck edge after the doily is attached to the shirt.

3 The next step is a very important one. Try on the shirt to test the size of the neck opening. It should be large enough to get your head through easily. If it is not large enough, staystitch in a larger circle around the neckline, cut away the shirt to the new stitching line, and try the shirt on again to test the opening. This is essential, because once the doily is stitched to the neck edge, most of the stretchiness of the neck opening will be lost.

4 Lay the doily over the neck hole and shoulders and plan the placement (Fig. 10-3). Carefully pin the doily in place on the shirt with many pins and sew the doily around the neck edge from the underside, stitching on top of the staystitching line. Cut away the center of the doily and test the size of the opening once again.

Figure 10-1: A plain T-shirt neckline is encircled with a doily and topped with a ribbon bow drawn through a casing.

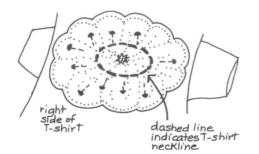

right side of T-shirt

dashed line indicates T-shirt neckline

Figure 10-3: Pin the doily over the T-shirt neck hole and shoulders.

5 Use the shirt's neck ribbing to make a neckline casing. Measure ¾" (2cm) down from the top folded edge of the ribbing and cut all the way around the ribbing as shown in Figure 10-4.

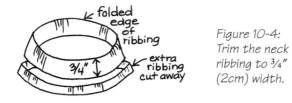

folded edge of ribbing

¾"

extra ribbing cut away

Figure 10-4: Trim the neck ribbing to ¾" (2cm) width.

Cut open the band of ribbing and press the cut edges inside the band (Fig. 10-5).

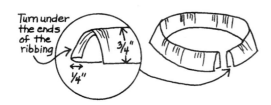

Turn under the ends of the ribbing

¾"

¼"

Figure 10-5: Cut the ribbing open, and then turn under the cut edges and press them.

6 With the short ends of the ribbing band at the shirt's center front, pin the long raw edges of the ribbing to the neck edge of the shirt so that the raw edges are even and the ribbing faces the right side of the shirt (Fig. 10-6). Sew or serge the ribbing to the shirt with a ¼" (6mm) seam allowance.

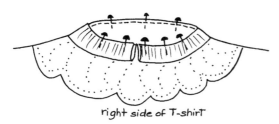

right side of T-shirt

Figure 10-6: Pin the ribbing to shirt's neckline, with the open short ends placed together at the center front.

7 Turn and press the seam allowance toward the shirt body on the wrong side of the garment. Topstitch the seam allowances to keep them in place. The topstitching will be hidden if you lift the doily and stitch the seam to the T-shirt only (Fig. 10-7).

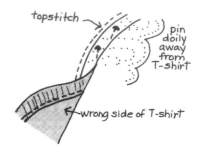

topstitch

pin doily away from T-shirt

wrong side of T-shirt

Figure 10-7: To create a hidden seam, topstitch the seam allowance to only the T-shirt, pinning the doily out of the way.

8 Borrowing an idea from a purchased T-shirt, I decided to make the neckline look neater by covering the back neck seam where part of the lace doily edge showed. I sewed narrow bias tape over the ribbing edge, lifting the doily out of the way and attaching the tape to the T-shirt fabric only. I added the bias tape along the back neck seam between the shoulder seams (Fig. 10-8).

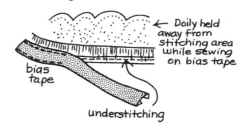

Wrong side of T-shirt back neckline

Doily held away from stitching area while sewing on bias tape

bias tape

understitching

Figure 10-8: Sew bias tape over the seam on the back neckline.

9 Thread the piece of ribbon or cord through the casing.

This feminine neck treatment adds an interesting detail to a plain T-shirt. If you like this idea, think about using fabric instead of a doily for the neckline. Chose a soft fabric that drapes well, such as rayon.

T-Shirt with Attached Vest 11

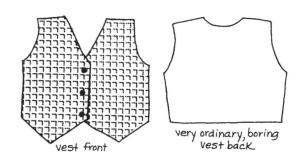

Figure 11-1: At the shoulder and side seams, separate the vest front from the back.

*C*ombine two garments in one if you like the look of a vest over a plain T-shirt (see p. 30). The vest is taken apart at the shoulder and side seams and only the vest front is sewn to the T-shirt. Most vest backs are plain, so you won't be eliminating anything interesting by removing the back. The vest front is trimmed with an applique and new buttons, to make a more interesting garment. I chose to applique a plaid vest. Appliqueing on plaid fabric was once not even considered to be an option, but it's acceptable now to break some of the rules and to experiment with new combinations and patterns.

SUPPLY LIST

1 PLAIN T-SHIRT

1 VEST

PAPER-BACKED FUSIBLE WEB

FABRICS FOR APPLIQUE

STABILIZER (OPTIONAL)

REPLACEMENT BUTTONS FOR VEST FRONT (OPTIONAL)

1 Let's work on the vest first. With the vest front buttoned, use a seam ripper to take apart the vest front and back at both the shoulder seams and the side seams (Fig. 11-1).

2 It's easier to add an applique to the vest before attaching the vest front to the T-shirt, but it can also be done after the vest is sewn on. If your vest is plaid—like the one I decorated—or printed, a solid-color applique can be very effective. I used Ultrasuede in solid colors to contrast with the dull plaid of the vest, for a pleasing effect. First trace the floral applique design found in Figure 11-3 (p. 31) onto paper-backed fusible web. Fuse the web to the Ultrasuede and cut the shapes from the fabric. Remove the paper backing from the appliques and fuse them to the vest front, being sure to use a press cloth to protect the suede fabric. Sew the appliques to vest with clear nylon thread, using a narrow blanket stitch for a nearly invisible stitching line.

3 After the vest has been trimmed, place it over the shirt front, lining up the shoulder seams first and then the side seams. Pin the entire vest front to the shirt, keeping the shoulder and side seam areas free of pins (Fig. 11-2).

Dotted lines show fold lines of vest seam allowances to line up with shoulder and side seams of T-shirt.

Figure 11-2: Pin the vest front to the T-shirt, lining up the seam folds on the vest with the T-shirt's shoulder and side seams.

T-Shirt with Attached Vest

Sew a vest front to a T-shirt to create a garment with a layered look. A floral applique cut from Ultrasuede decorates the plain vest fronts, and interesting buttons replace the vest's original ordinary ones.

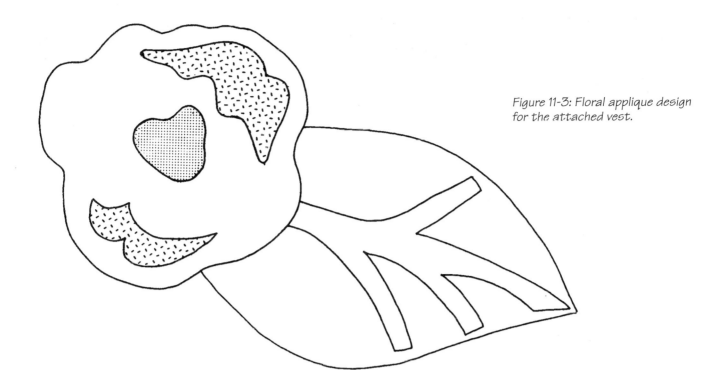

Figure 11-3: Floral applique design for the attached vest.

4 Turn under and press the seam allowances of the vest at the shoulders so that they meet the shoulder seams of the T-shirt. Do the same with the seam allowances of the vest's sides. Since many T-shirts do not have side seams, you'll be lining up the vest sides with the folds that form at the shirt's sides. Press the folds forming at the shirt's sides so that you will have clear stitching guides.

5 Unbutton the vest fronts and remove some of the pins holding the vest to the shirt so that you can sew the vest to the shirt at the shoulders. The seam will be hidden if you stitch inside the vest, using the pressed fold line on the vest as the stitching guide. Line up the fold with the shoulder seam of the shirt. Use the same procedure for attaching the vest to the T-shirt's side seams or fold line (Fig. 11-4).

6 Now that the vest is attached permanently to the shirt, look at its buttons and decide if they should be changed. I enjoyed selecting three very different buttons to add to my vest. Make sure that the buttons will fit the buttonholes if you want to be able to wear the garment with the vest closed (Fig. 11-5).

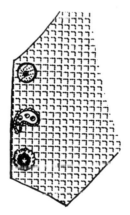

Figure 11-5: Use interesting buttons to trim the vest.

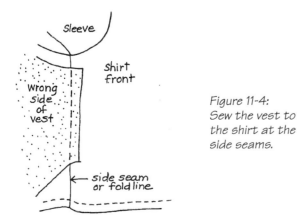

Figure 11-4: Sew the vest to the shirt at the side seams.

Sleeve

Shirt front

Wrong side of vest

side seam or fold line

T-Shirt Front Yokes with Fringe or Lace

12

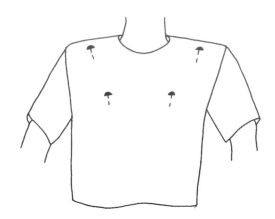

Figure 12-1: Mark the sides of the yoke and the bustline with pins.

Add a fabric yoke to a T-shirt front for added color. Trim the yoke with fringe for a western look; a more feminine style can be created with lace. A yoke trims the garment's neckline, which frames the head and face and draws the eye upward.

T-Shirt with Fringed Yoke

Make the fringe or use purchased fringe to trim the lower edge of the yoke. Tie beads to the ends of the fringe for added interest.

SUPPLY LIST

1 PLAIN T-SHIRT

TISSUE WRAPPING PAPER

1/4 YD. (23CM) PAPER-BACKED FUSIBLE WEB

1/4 YD. (23CM) FABRIC FOR YOKE

ONE 8 1/2 X 11" (22 X 28CM) PIECE OF WHITE PAPER

1 BALL OF COTTON CROCHET THREAD (OR YARN OR CORD) FOR FRINGE

1/4 YD. (23CM) STABILIZER

SEVERAL BEADS TO DECORATE FRINGE (OPTIONAL)

1 Try on the T-shirt, adding shoulder pads if they will be worn with the garment, and mark the outer edges of the yoke. If the T-shirt has a dropped shoulder line, you may not want the yoke to extend all the way to the sleeve seam. Also mark the bustline. Most yokes look flattering if they end above the bustline (Fig. 12-1).

2 Fold the shirt in half along the center front and pin the shoulder seams together. Line up the folded shirt on a folded piece of tissue paper as shown in Figure 12-2 and make the yoke pattern, using the pin-tracing technique described in Section 6. For the shirt in the photo, the yoke pattern was made 1/2" (1.3cm) below the neckline edge and 1" (2.5cm) below the shoulder seam. The yoke is 4 1/2" (11.5cm) long at the rounded front portion, and the shorter shoulder sections are 3 1/2" (9cm) long. Of course, you can make the yoke for your shirt any size you'd like.

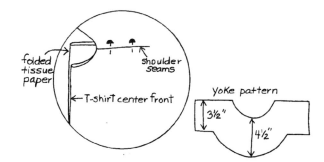

Figure 12-2: Fold the shirt on the center front line and place it on tissue paper to make the yoke pattern.

3 After cutting out the tissue pattern for the yoke, lay it on the shirt front to test the placement and size of the yoke. Trace the final pattern on paper-backed fusible web, fuse the pattern to the wrong side of the yoke fabric, and cut out the yoke.

T-Shirt Front Yokes with Fringe or Lace

Add a fabric yoke to a T-shirt and enhance it with extra trim. On the gold T-shirt, a brown imitation suede yoke is decorated with fringe made of crochet thread. Small beads are tied to several of the fringe strands. On the V-neck T-shirt, the print fabric yoke (P&B Fabrics) is outlined with ecru lace trim. A dimensional flower and leaf applique adds extra texture to the yoke.

4 Peel off the paper backing and partially fuse the yoke to the shirt, leaving the bottom edge loose so that you can insert the fringe. But first, of course, you must make the fringe.

5 Fold the piece of white paper in half lengthwise and cut it apart at the fold (Fig. 12-3). Then fold each piece in half lengthwise, overlap them by ½" (1.3cm), and tape the two pieces together at the short ends.

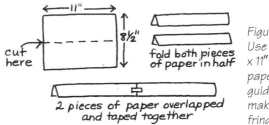

Figure 12-3: Use an 8½" x 11" piece of paper as a guide for making the fringe.

6 Wrap the crochet thread (or string or yarn) around the long paper strip. Wrap loosely so that the paper does not curl. Stitch along one long edge of the yarn-wrapped paper to secure the yarn (Fig. 12-4). I used the wide machine stitch illustrated.

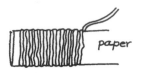

paper

utility stitch sewn at top edge of paper with yarn wrapped around

Figure 12-4: Wrap the paper strip with yarn and sew near one edge of the paper to hold the fringe together.

7 Along the opposite edge from the stitching, cut the folds of the yarn to create fringe. If you want some strands of the fringe longer for tying on beads, cut those strands from the back before cutting on the fold. Then tear away the paper. It will be difficult (or impossible) to tear away the small width of paper at the top edge of the fringe, so leave it in the stitching (Fig. 12-5).

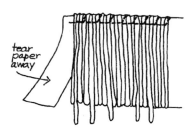

tear paper away

Figure 12-5: Some pieces of the fringe are cut longer for knotting or beads. After cutting the rest of the fringe along the fold opposite the stitching, tear away the paper.

8 Place the stitched edge of the fringe beneath the lower edge of the yoke and pin it carefully in place (Fig. 12-6). You may prefer to straight stitch the fringe in place on the shirt before sewing around the edges of the yoke. For stitching along all of the edges of the yoke, I chose a wide stitch, which secured the fabric and fringe and added another detail to the shirt. Use a stabilizer on the wrong side of the T-shirt, if needed, while stitching. Add extra trim to the shirt yoke if you think it needs more decoration.

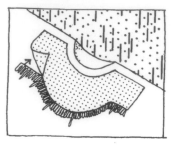

Figure 12-6: The sewn edge of the fringe is inserted beneath the lower edge of the fabric yoke.

T-Shirt with Lace-Trimmed Yoke

The shape of the yoke on the teal T-shirt on page 33 was dictated by the V-neck of the garment (Fig 12-7). This shirt has a decorative lace trim along the bottom of the yoke; a narrower lace covers the sides and neck edges of the yoke.

Figure 12-7: The yoke on the V-neck T-shirt was trimmed with lace and a flower.

SUPPLY LIST

1 PLAIN V-NECK T-SHIRT

TISSUE WRAPPING PAPER

½ YD. (46CM) PAPER-BACKED FUSIBLE WEB

½ YD. (46CM) FABRIC FOR YOKE

1 YD. (0.95M) *EACH OF 2 DIFFERENT WIDTH LACES*

FABRIC PIECES FOR FLOWER AND LEAF TRIM

¼" (6MM) STRIPS OF PAPER-BACKED FUSIBLE WEB.

1 BUTTON FOR FLOWER CENTER

1 Follow Steps 1–3 for "T-Shirt with Fringed Yoke," earlier in this section, this time creating a V-shaped 3"–wide (7.5cm) yoke.

2 Remove the paper backing from the fabric yoke and fuse the yoke to the shirt front.

3 Use lace to cover all the edges of the yoke. Use a medium zigzag stitch to attach the lace. Note that the larger-width lace goes along the outside and the narrower lace goes along the inside and shoulders of the yoke.

4 To make the dimensional flower applique, cut a 3½″ (9cm) square of cotton fabric. Fuse strips of paper-backed fusible web to all four edges of the square on the wrong side of the fabric (Fig. 12-8). Peel off the paper; turn the edges under, overlapping them at the corners; and fuse them in place to the back of the fabric.

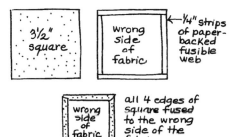

Figure 12-8: Turn under and fuse the edges of the 3 ½″ (9cm) square of fabric.

5 Fold the square twice, as illustrated in Figure 12-9.

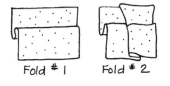

Figure 12-9: Take up a fold in the middle of the square, first horizontally and then vertically.

The two folds will cross each other near the center of the square. Pin the folds in place and sew a button over the center (Fig. 12-10).

Figure 12-10: Sew a button at the center to hold the folds in place.

6 Using the leaf pattern shown in Figure 12-11, cut two leaves from nonfraying fabric; I used Ultrasuede. Make a pleat at the top edge of each leaf, as shown in Figure 12-12. Sew the top of the leaves to the flower center. Sew or pin the dimensional flower applique to the T-shirt yoke.

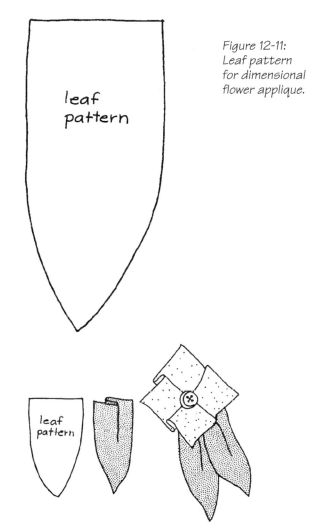

Figure 12-11: Leaf pattern for dimensional flower applique.

Figure 12-12: Fold the top edges of the two leaves and add them to the flower.

T-shirt yokes are easy to add, and they drastically change the garment— from ordinary to original!

T-Shirt Hood with Reverse Applique 13

Serge or zigzag stitch the two long edges to prevent the fabric from fraying. I used fusible thread in the upper looper of the serger, and then serged the fabric with the right side of the fabric up (Fig. 13-2). (The other three threads on the serger were standard serging thread.) With the fusible thread on the right side of the fabric, the fabric strip edges can be fused to the inside of the hood. If you don't have a serger, apply narrow strips of fusible web along the long edges of the fabric piece so that you'll be able to fuse it to the hood.

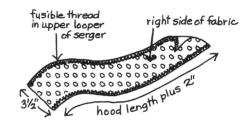

fusible thread in upper looper of serger

right side of fabric

3½"

hood length plus 2"

Figure 13-2: Hood applique fabric with serged edges.

*A*dd style and interest to the hood of a beach coverup with reverse applique and multicolored fabric. Whether the hood is worn on the head or down over the shoulders, the reverse applique designs are sure to be an attractive detail.

SUPPLY LIST

1 PLAIN KNIT BEACH COVERUP OR T-SHIRT WITH HOOD

3½"-WIDE (9CM) BAND OF FABRIC FOR INSIDE OF HOOD (SELECT A FABRIC THAT LOOKS GOOD ON BOTH THE RIGHT AND WRONG SIDES)

3½"-WIDE (9CM) BAND OF A DIFFERENT FABRIC FOR A DOUBLE-LAYER INSIDE OF HOOD (OPTIONAL)

STRIPS OF FUSIBLE WEB

FUSIBLE THREAD FOR SERGING (OPTIONAL)

1 Measure the distance around the edge of the hood (Fig. 13-1), add 2" (5cm), and cut the fabric band to that length.

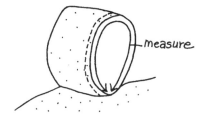

measure

Figure 13-1: Measure the outer edge of the hood opening and add 2" (5cm) to the measurement.

T-Shirt Hood with Reverse Applique

A novel place to trim a hooded T-shirt is inside the hood. Here reverse applique adds color and interest to the edges of the hood (shirt by Max e.b.).

Figure 13-4: Sea and summer applique designs.

2 And that's the next step: Place the fabric strip inside the hood with the right side of the fabric against the wrong side of the hood. I positioned my fabric strip close to the outside edge of the hood, lining it up with the folded-over hem allowance in the hood (Fig. 13-3). Fuse the strip in place.

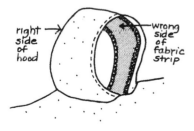

Figure 13-3: Applique fabric strip inside hood with wrong side of fabric showing.

3 Trace the sea and summer design shapes from Figure 13-4 onto paper and cut out the shapes.

4 Using a water-soluble marker, trace the shapes in random order around the hood opening. Be sure that you have drawn the designs so that they fall within the edges of the fabric strip attached to the inside of the hood.

5 Before sewing, add extra insurance to the fabric strip placement inside the hood by pinning the strip to the hood in a few places. Use a short straight stitch to sew along the traced lines on the hood (Fig. 13-5).

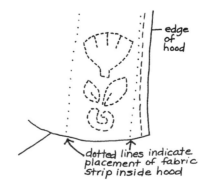

Figure 13-5: Sew around the design shapes that you traced onto the right side of the hood.

6 Now it's time to cut away the hood fabric inside the stitching lines to reveal the fabric strip beneath. *Carefully* cut a hole inside each design shape and trim away the fabric to approximately ⅛" (3mm) from the sewing lines (Fig. 13-6). The knit fabric of the hood will not ravel or fray, and with laundering and wear, the fabric edge will curl and add extra interest to the edges of the designs.

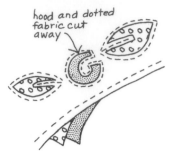

Figure 13-8: Cut through just the hood to reveal the first layer of fabric, and through both the hood and first fabric to reveal the second fabric.

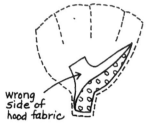

Figure 13-6: Cut away the hood fabric inside the stitching lines to expose the fabric band.

To add more trim to the beach coverup, consider repeating the sea and summer design shapes elsewhere on the garment.

Bright Idea

The pelican-billed applique scissors (see Fig. 4-3) look unusual, but they certainly are handy. I value their very sharp points and usually reach for them when I cut away the fabric in reverse applique.

7 Another way to do reverse applique is to add two layers of fabric to the wrong side of the garment (Fig. 13-7).

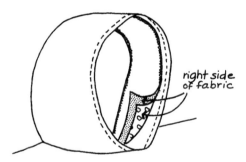

Figure 13-7: Two layers of fabric positioned in the hood and ready for reverse applique.

Select lightweight fabrics to avoid adding too much stiffness or weight to the hood. Serge the fabric edges together to make one fabric unit to attach to the inside of the hood. Fuse the long edges of the fabric piece in place inside the hood, and trace the design shapes on the outside of the hood. After sewing around the design shapes, you can cut some of the shapes through the knit layer only and others through the knit layer and one of the fabric layers to reveal the second fabric (Fig. 13-8). Your hood will then be decorated with two different fabrics.

Overlay Applique Tunic

14

Figure 14-1: The squares in this printed fabric are easy to cover with overlay applique.

R eview the printed garments in your closet for a possible transformation with overlay applique. By stitching fabric over the shapes on the printed fabric, you'll add dimension, texture, and interest to the garment. It's my preference to select prints with shapes that are easy to trace and sew around, like the squares in the tunic shown in the photo on page 40, but there are no limits to the shapes you can select for overlay applique. The tunic I used was one that I sewed myself that needed some interesting detail. The applique fabric shown in the photo is a shiny, sequined material.

Figure 14-2: Cover the design area with a piece of tracing paper and trace the design from the fabric.

SUPPLY LIST

1 PRINTED TUNIC

TRACING PAPER

¼ YD. (23CM) PAPER-BACKED FUSIBLE WEB

FABRIC FOR OVERLAY APPLIQUES

¼ YD. (23CM) TEAR-AWAY STABILIZER

1 Study the print of the garment you've chosen to decorate and select the printed areas you'd like to cover with appliques (Fig. 14-1). Make this decision while wearing the garment to avoid placing designs in unflattering locations.

2 Trace the design shapes directly from the fabric onto the tracing paper. Write the word *front* in the center of each of the designs you trace (Fig. 14-2).

3 Turn the tracing paper templates over (the word *front* will now be reversed) and trace the shapes onto the paper side of the paper-backed fusible web (Fig. 14-3). Fuse the piece of web with the designs drawn on it to the wrong side of the fabric chosen for the overlay, and cut out the shapes.

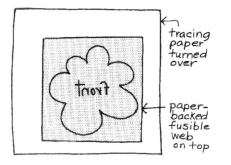

Figure 14-3: Turn the tracing paper template over and trace the reversed shape onto the paper-backed fusible web.

Overlay Applique Tunic and Corner-Trimmed Tunic
Tunics of longer lengths present interesting options for decorating. Corner trim is added to the pink tunic at the hemline and the opposite shoulder (Section 15). Lycra fabrics are used for the appliques, which are sewn on with Sliver metallic thread by Sulky. On a tunic made from print fabric, design shapes found in the print can be traced and cut out of another fabric to create overlay appliques (Section 14). For the overlay applique on the brightly colored tunic shown, rectangles of black sequined fabric (shown strewn above the tunic as well as sewn to it) are used to highlight the windowpane print.

4 Once you remove the paper backing from the designs, they are ready to be fused to the garment. Position the appliques exactly on top of the areas you traced, and fuse them. Place stabilizer on the wrong side of the garment underneath the area to be appliqued, and stitch around the edges of the design shapes to sew them to the tunic. Depending on the fabric you've chosen for the overlays, you may prefer to use clear thread or thread to match the overlay fabric so that the stitching is not a prominent part of the design. If the overlay fabric will not fray, straight stitching or a very narrow zigzag stitch is a good choice for securing the edges to the garment. Use a satin stitch if you want to prevent the overlay fabric from fraying. Or you could use a straight stitch on a fabric that frays and incorporate the frayed edges into the overall design.

5 Remove the stabilizer from the back of the garment after the stitching is complete.

Now when you wear your tunic, different portions of the printed fabric will stand out, giving a new dimension to the print. This easy technique adds unexpected pizzazz and eliminates the need to select an applique design—it's there in the printed fabric, just waiting for you to discover and highlight.

Corner-Trimmed Tunic
15

SUPPLY LIST

1 PLAIN TUNIC WITH SHIRTTAILS

¼ YD. (23CM) PAPER-BACKED FUSIBLE WEB

FABRIC PIECES FOR THE CORNER DESIGNS

¼ YD. (23CM) TEAR-AWAY STABILIZER

C hoose a tunic with shirttails for this design application. One shirttail corner is trimmed, and a matching design is placed at the opposite shoulder. If you don't mind two designs at hip level, you could trim both shirttail edges. I used Lycra fabrics to make the design shapes I added to my tunic (Fig. 15-1).

1 I suggest that you test the size and location of the designs before you cut the appliques from the fabric. Make individual paper applique shapes or make a pattern of the entire design area. Pin the paper appliques to the garment and then try it on. I used the applique pattern given in Figure 15-3 (p. 42) "as is" for the bottom corner of the tunic. I found that I needed to shorten one bar on the applique design when I applied it to the shoulder area (Fig. 15-2). Otherwise the outline of the design would have been located within the folds created when the garment is worn. If you expect to wear shoulder pads, make sure they are in place when you are planning the shoulder trim. Shoulder pads can affect the design location.

Figure 15-1: Add matching applique designs to the diagonal corners of a knit tunic.

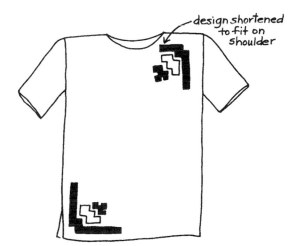

Figure 15-2: Tunic with one bar of corner design shortened for use on shoulder.

2 Trace the design shapes from Figure 15-3 onto paper-backed fusible web. Cut out the shapes. Fuse the web to the wrong side of the applique fabrics, and cut the shapes from the fabric.

3 Remove the paper backing from the shapes and fuse them in the correct positions on the garment. Pin or attach the stabilizer to the wrong side of the tunic beneath the design areas.

4 Any kind of sewing thread will work to sew the shapes to the tunic, but I chose a metallic foil thread, which is a shiny ribbonlike thread that is more reflective than regular metallic thread. To use this thread, the spool must be placed on a vertical spool holder rather than a horizontal one. Use a size 80/12 embroidery or topstitching needle on your sewing machine or a size 80 or 90 needle. In the bobbin, use a thread that matches the color of the top thread; a metallic, rayon, or fine sewing thread will work well. Decrease the top ten-

sion on the machine. You will need to sew slowly. If you haven't used metallic foil thread before, experiment on test fabric before you sew on the tunic.

5 For this project, consider using a standard stitch in a new way. I used the blind hem stitch and varied the direction of the points, as shown in Figure 15-4. Experiment on your test fabric to determine the best stitch width and length for your applique.

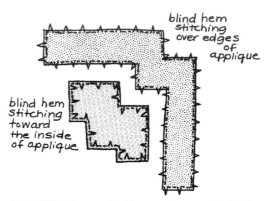

blind hem stitching over edges of applique

blind hem stitching toward the inside of applique

Figure 15-4: Blind hem stitching can be used in both directions to add variety to the appliques.

6 After the stitching is complete, remove the stabilizer and press the design. Metallic foil thread should be ironed on low heat.

Placing appliques on opposite corners of the garment draws the eye in a diagonal line from the shoulder to the hem. This placement is flattering because it does not emphasize the body's width.

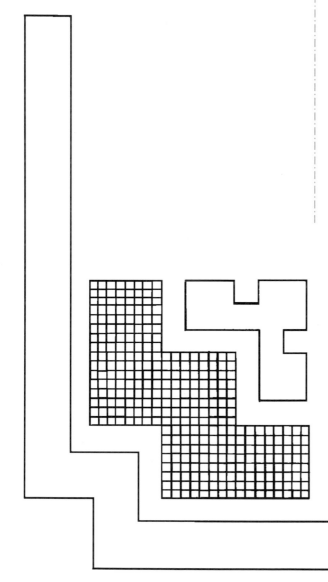

Figure 15-3: Applique pattern for corner trim.

Tunic with Lace Medley & Beads

16

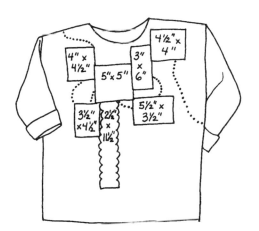

Figure 16-1: Location and sizes of the lace patches.

Select samples from your lace fabric collection for the denim tunic shown on page 44. The pieces can also be salvaged from old dresser scarves, doilies, and tablecloths. After the lace is sewn on, a strand of cross-locked beads is couched over the top. Cross-locked glass beads are specially designed so that the strand does not fall apart when it is cut.

SUPPLY LIST

1 PLAIN TUNIC

ASSORTMENT OF LACE FOR THE DECORATIVE PATCHES

¼ YD. (23CM) PAPER-BACKED FUSIBLE WEB

TISSUE WRAPPING PAPER

2 YD. (1.85M) CROSS-LOCKED GLASS BEADS

ASSORTMENT OF BEADS, RIBBON, AND OTHER TRIM (OPTIONAL)

¾ YD. (69CM) TEAR-AWAY STABILIZER (OPTIONAL)

1 Use the tunic in the photo to plan the location of the lace patches; Figure 16-1 shows the sizes of the patches I used on my tunic. Or plan your own design to show off the different laces you will be using. The extra length of a tunic allows a larger display area; consider adding pieces in vertical lines to emphasize your height rather than width! Mark the bustline before laying out the design to avoid awkward placement of the design.

2 Cut the lace pieces slightly larger than you want the finished patches to be. If a piece of lace is too sheer, use two pieces of the same lace together.

3 Cut pieces of paper-backed fusible web the same size as the lace pieces. Place the lace, right side down, on top of tissue paper and cover the lace with a piece of paper-backed fusible web. Fuse. The tissue paper will absorb the extra fusible web and will protect your ironing board. Work on different areas of the tissue paper so you don't mess up your iron. Discard the used tissue paper.

4 Trim the edges of the lace with the web still attached. Remove the paper and position the lace on the tunic. Before fusing the lace to the shirt, place a single sheet of tissue paper over the lace appliques. Again, the tissue will absorb the excess fusible web; discard the used tissue paper.

5 Depending on the tunic's fabric, you may need to add stabilizer to the wrong side of the garment before stitching along the edges of the lace. On my tunic, I found that stabilizer was not necessary, because the denim fabric was stable and the stitch I used was a narrow zigzag.

Tunic with Lace Medley and Beads

Showcase your collection of lace fabrics and trims on a plain tunic. Over the lace, sew a string of cross-locked beads and sprinkle on a variety of buttons and metallic studs. This tunic, by Sunbelt Sportswear, no longer looks ordinary or plain.

6 A narrow zigzag is a good choice for stitching the applique because it hides in the edges of the lace. The colors of the thread I used also helped hide the stitching. The top thread was ecru to blend with the lace and the bobbin thread was blue to match fhe garment. Press the tunic after you're finished sewing.

7 Now plan the placement of the string of beads. Maneuver the beads around the shirt front until you like the arrangement and then draw a guide line with a water-soluble marker.

8 Several kinds of presser feet can be used to sew on the beads. Look at the feet that came with your sewing machine and select a foot with a space between the presser foot toes, or a hemmer foot. Another good choice is the Pearls 'N Piping Foot by C.J. Enterprises; it has a large groove under both the front and back of the foot (Fig. 16-2).

Figure 16-2: This specialty presser foot is used for sewing cross-locked beads and other trim.

9 Once you've chosen a presser foot, set the machine for a medium zigzag stitch. Practice sewing the beads onto test fabric before sewing them onto your tunic. Adjust the stitch width and choice of presser foot as needed to get the results you want. (Refer to "What is Couching" on page 56 for additional tips on this technique.) After you're done experimenting, rip out the stitching to release the string of beads.

10 I placed the end of the string of beads into the tunic's shoulder seam to imitate ready-to-wear garments. You'll need to cut open only one or two stitches of the shoulder seam to insert the end of the string of beads. Pull the end of the beads to the edge of the seam allowance inside the tunic and anchor the beads with stitching (Fig. 16-3). If you do not want to insert the beads into the seam, simply backstitch to anchor the end onto the tunic.

Right Side of Tunic

Wrong Side of Tunic

Shoulder Seam

anchoring stitches for beads

Shoulder Seam

Figure 16-3: The end of the string of beads is inserted through the shoulder seam and then secured. After sewing, trim away any beads that extend past the stitching.

11 Following the line you drew on the tunic in Step 7, sew on the beads. Try not to pull on the beads, because this will pucker the tunic fabric. Anchor the end of the string of beads into the side seam, as I did, or onto the top of the tunic.

12 After the beads are in place, add an assortment of beads, buttons, studs, ribbons, or other trim to suit your personal taste.

Bright Idea

It helps to know the measurements of nearby items or areas in your sewing room. When measuring my closet door for a bulletin board, I discovered that it is 36" (91.5cm) wide. It's a handy measure to have next to my ironing board.

Patriotic & Golf Tank Tops

17

Figure 17-2: Location of applique triangles.

T ank tops can be trimmed to reflect midsummer fun. Wear the patriotic tank to a Fourth of July picnic. The golf top will help you stay cool and look sharp on the links.

Patriotic Tank Top

For someone like me, living in the far north in Minnesota, a tank top is a Fourth of July kind of garment, mostly because that's often the first (and only) day it's warm enough to wear one (a slight exaggeration!). With that in mind, I created this patriotic design, which can also be interpreted in other colors. I chose faded shades of red, white, and blue.

SUPPLY LIST

1 PLAIN TANK TOP IN A COLOR THAT WILL COORDINATE WITH RED, WHITE, AND BLUE DECORATIONS

ONE 6" (15CM) SQUARE OF PAPER-BACKED FUSIBLE WEB

ONE 6" (15CM) SQUARE OF BLUE ULTRASUEDE

ONE 6" (15CM) SQUARE EACH OF RED AND WHITE/OFF WHITE COTTON FABRICS FOR FRINGE

1 Try on the tank top to test the location of the design. Make three paper triangles, traced from Figure 17-1 (p. 47). Pin the triangles onto the tank to determine their best locations. Check that the line created by the upper edge of the triangle patterns follows the neckline curve of the shirt; adjust the triangles if necessary (Fig. 17-2).

Your tank may have wider shoulder straps than the one I used, so you may prefer to add additional triangles to encircle the neckline. Once you've decided on your design layout, trace the triangles onto the shirt with a water-soluble marker.

2 Trace three triangle shapes onto paper-backed fusible web. Fuse the shapes to the wrong side of the blue Ultrasuede, and cut out the shapes, following the lines you drew. Cut out the star shapes from the center of the triangles, following the pattern shown in Figure 17-1, or leave the triangles solid.

3 For this shirt, you will tear the red and white fabrics used for the fringe instead of cutting them. From the red and white fabrics, tear four strips ½" (1.3cm) or wider. Tie a knot near one end of each strip (Fig. 17-3).

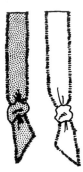

Figure 17-3: Tear the fabric fringe instead of cutting it; then put a knot in one end of each strip.

4 Remove the paper backing from the Ultra-suede triangles and place the shapes around the neckline of the tank top, following the lines you drew in Step 1. Insert the unknotted end of the fabric strips beneath the edge of the center triangle, as shown in Figure 17-4, making sure that the edges of fabric strips do not show through the cutout star. Pin the triangles and fringe strips to the shirt and try it on again to make sure the length of the fringe is flattering. Add fringe to each of the other triangles, if you wish.

Patriotic and Golf Tank Tops

Add style to plain tank tops with the applique and fringe options featured here. The golf motif applique on the pink tank top is cut from Ultrasuede and sewn on with clear nylon thread for a nearly invisible stitching line. On the ivory tank top, the blue Ultrasuede triangles have stars cut from the centers, while fringe made from frayed strips of cotton fabric trims the center triangle.

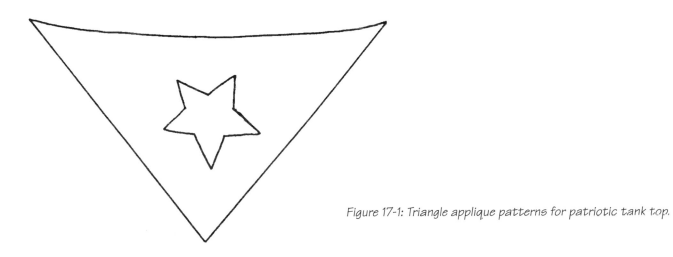

Figure 17-1: Triangle applique patterns for patriotic tank top.

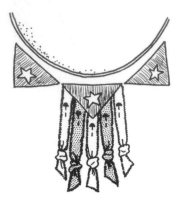

Figure 17-4: The ends of the fringe are inserted beneath the center triangle before fusing.

5 When you are satisfied with the fringe length, fuse the triangles onto the shirt, using a press cloth to protect the surface of the Ultrasuede. The ends of the fringe will be fused under the center triangle.

6 To finish your tank, sew around each of the triangles to secure them to the garment. I selected a decorative machine stitch for this garment, but straight stitching works well with Ultrasuede

Even after washing, the torn fringe will look good. You may want to trim away the extra threads that loosen off the sides of the fabric strips. Press the fringe after you launder the shirt for a crisp look. Try this idea in an entirely different color scheme. It would also work well on a round-neck T-shirt.

Tank Top with Golf Applique

Turn a plain tank top into a garment just right for the golf course. I used Ultrasuede for the appliques and placed the design off-center. Consider enlarging or reducing the design for use on other garments.

SUPPLY LIST

1 PLAIN TANK TOP

¼ YD. (23CM) PAPER-BACKED FUSIBLE WEB

SMALL PIECES OF FABRIC FOR APPLIQUES

ONE 9″ (23CM) SQUARE OF STABILIZER

FABRIC PAINT (OPTIONAL)

PAPER PUNCH, LEATHER TOOLING CIRCLE PUNCH, OR HOLE CUTTER FOR AN EYELET BUTTONHOLE (OPTIONAL)

1 Before cutting the applique shapes from fabric, test the design using paper. Trace the outline of the design onto paper, and cut it out (Fig. 17-5). Pin the paper applique to the tank top and try on the shirt to check the size and location of the design. Do you like the design off-center or is it more pleasing in another location? You will save yourself time and expense by using paper instead of fabric to plan the design for your top. Once you've decided on the placement of your design, trace the shapes onto the shirt using a washable marker.

2 The design in Figure 17-5 is drawn as a mirror image so that you can trace it directly onto paper-backed fusible web. Trace the designs onto the paper-backed web and cut out the shapes. Fuse the web to the wrong sides of the fabrics you have chosen for the design. Cut out the designs from the fabric. Note that I included the number 9 in case you prefer 9 holes of golf instead of 18.

3 No matter which number you choose, cut it out from the flag shape, following the outside line of the number (Fig. 17-6). From the waste pieces of the flag fabric, cut out the small circles to complete the number 8 (or number 9). Remove the backing from these pieces and fuse them onto the tank top, following the lines you drew with washable marker. The garment color will show through the flag and become the color of the number. If you prefer another color to show through, place an additional piece of fused fabric beneath the number area before fusing the number "middles" to the shirt.

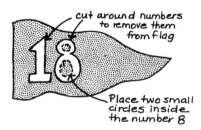

Figure 17-6: Cut the numbers from the flag and add small circles of the flag fabric to complete the number 8.

4 To add more detail to the golf ball, paint dots or make small holes in the ball with a paper punch, leather tooling circle punch, or the hole cutter for an eyelet buttonhole (Fig. 17-7).

Figure 17-5: Golf applique designs, with writing reversed for easy tracing.

Once the golf ball looks realistic enough for you, fuse it and the rest of the design onto the shirt. Remember to peel off the paper backing before you fuse the shapes and to use the lines you drew in Step 1 as a guide for design placement.

Figure 17-7: Golf ball with dots added.

5 Place and attach the stabilizer to the wrong side of the tank beneath the design area before sewing. If you have used nonfraying fabric for the appliques, sew around the edges using a clear thread as the top thread and a bobbin thread to match the color of the tank top. Use a straight stitch or a narrow blanket stitch for an invisible applique. Figure 17-8 is a guide for stitching the golf appliques. First sew around the golf club, then the flag, and finally the flag pole. This stitching order follows the general rule of sewing the shapes farthest in the background first. In the same manner, first sew around the vertical golf tee and then sew around the golf ball and grass. Don't forget to sew around the edges of the horizontal golf tee.

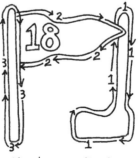

Figure 17-8: Guide to sewing around the golf appliques. The numbers indicate the order of stitching and the arrows, the direction.

Numbers indicate stitching order

6 After the stitching is complete, pull the top threads to the back of the tank and knot. Remove the stabilizer, and you're ready to wear this newly trimmed garment on your next golf outing.

Vests
Part Four

Quick-Change Vest 18

I t takes only a few minutes to convert a plain vest to a designer wearable like the vest shown on page 52. Then, if you'd like to restore the plain vest, the additions are easy to remove and can be applied to another garment. My favorite kind of vest for this project is a man's suit vest. Often you will be able to find one hidden in the back of a man's closet as part of a three piece suit that he no longer wears.

SUPPLY LIST

1 PLAIN VEST

BUTTON COVERS (ONE FOR EACH BUTTON ON THE VEST)

ONE 3 X 5″ (7.5 X 12.5CM) INDEX CARD

ONE 5 X 8″ (12.5 X 20.5CM) PIECE OF FABRIC OR ONE DOILY, 5 TO 8″ (12.5 TO 20.5CM) IN DIAMETER

ONE DOILY, 3 TO 4″ (7.5 TO 10CM) IN DIAMETER

ONE PAIR OF POST-STYLE PIERCED EARRINGS (TO COORDINATE WITH THE VEST)

1 A set of button covers is a wardrobe investment not only for this vest project but for other clothing as well (Fig. 18-1). Because the covers generally enlarge the existing button by a good amount, you must add the covers either to the unbuttoned vest, which is worn open, or the buttoned vest, which remains closed.

Button Cover
Front and Back Views

Figure 18-1: Button covers slide over the existing buttons to change the look of the garment.

2 Fold the index card in half along the 5″ (12.5cm) side to make the base for a pocket insert. Make the insert from a piece of fabric or a medium-size doily. If you choose fabric, like I did, fold the piece in half lengthwise. Sew the 8″ (20.5cm) raw edges together with a gathering seam (Fig. 18-2).

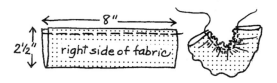

Figure 18-2: Gather the folded fabric along the 8″ (20.5cm) raw edges.

Pull the threads to gather the strip of fabric, and then distribute the gathers evenly. Pin the folded ends of the strip so that they are even with the outside edges of the folded index card. Sew across the fold on the index card to attach the fabric (Fig. 18-3). Knot the gathering threads to secure them before trimming the threads.

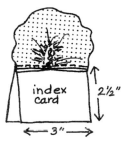

Figure 18-3: Sew the gathered strip to the folded edge of the index card.

Quick-Change Vest

I rescued this vest from a no-longer-worn man's suit and quickly trimmed it with removable accents. The vest features a pocket insert of gathered fabric, doily trim attached with pierced earrings, and button covers that transform the ordinary vest buttons.

3 To make the insert from the doily, fold the doily in half, gather it together at the center, distribute the folds, and sew the folded center of the doily to the folded index card (Fig. 18-4).

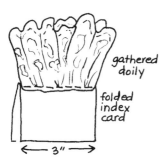

Figure 18-4: The complete gathered doily pocket insert.

gathered doily

folded index card

← 3" →

4 For another accent of trim, use a small doily with one or two pierced earrings as a center-piece. Fold a small tuck in the center of the doily and sew the tuck in place. Attach the folded doily to the vest with at least one post-style earring (Fig. 18-5). This is a good way to use an earring that no longer has a mate. Larger earrings hold the trim in place well. Since the earring's post will be passing through several layers of fabric, it usually won't be poking into your skin when you wear the vest. But do pay attention to how far the post extends past the wrong side of the vest front and make sure that it's long enough to hold the trim in place securely.

Figure 18-5: The folded doily is secured to the vest with two post-type pierced earrings.

If you make a variety of pocket inserts, you'll have even more selections for your quick-change vest. Just in case the vest's original owner wants to reclaim his vest, the decorations can be easily removed. Try these ideas to make a quick-change jacket too.

Bright Idea

When buying button covers, check their weight first. Some covers are very heavy and will affect the way that the front of a garment hangs.

Vest with Ultrasuede Squares & Yarn Couching

19

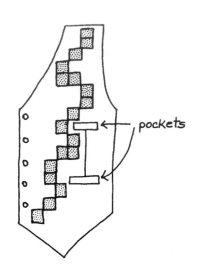

Figure 19-1: This applique design was planned around the vest's pocket openings.

An unworn vest from a man's three-piece suit becomes a sharp wardrobe addition thanks to squares of Ultrasuede and yarn attached by couching. Only one side of the vest is trimmed for this project, but the same technique can be applied to both sides.

SUPPLY LIST

1 VEST

1/4 YD. (23CM) PAPER-BACKED FUSIBLE WEB

ULTRASUEDE TO MAKE EIGHTEEN 1 1/2" (4CM) SQUARES

1/4 YD. (23CM) TEAR-AWAY STABILIZER

2 YD. (1.85M) OF YARN FOR COUCHING

1 Draw eighteen 1 1/2" (4cm) squares (or a number of your choice) onto paper-backed fusible web, and fuse them to the wrong side of the Ultrasuede. Cut out the squares, remove the paper backing, and plan the layout of the squares on the vest.

2 Use the design on the vest in the photo and in Figure 19-1, or plan your own. If the vest has pockets, you might begin laying out the design to the side and above the pocket openings. Or ignore the pockets and place the squares anywhere. Once the pattern layout looks good to you, carefully place a press cloth over the design area and fuse the Ultrasuede squares to the vest.

3 Place the stabilizer on the wrong side of the vest's front before you begin to sew. (If the vest front is lined, attach the stabilizer to the lining and sew through all the layers.) Due to the nonfraying edge of Ultrasuede, you can simply straight stitch the squares in place. You might want to choose one of your sewing machine's decorative stitches. I used black thread and a blanket stitch to attach the squares on my vest (Fig. 19-2). The blanket stitch is one of my favorites, and most sewing machines offer some version of it. The blanket stitch works well on nonfraying fabrics.

blanket stitch

Figure 19-2: The blanket stitch was used to secure the applique squares.

Vest with Ultrasuede Squares and Yarn Couching

On this man's vest, squares of Ultrasuede are stitched in place and variegated chenille yarn is sewn (couched) over the squares and on the vest to enhance the design.

4 Do not tear away the stabilizer when you are finished sewing down the squares. You'll need it while you're couching the yarn.

5 Before applying the couching to the vest, read "What Is Couching?" in this section and practice the technique on scrap fabric. Plan and draw the couching design on the vest. The pinstripes on my vest served as a guide for stitching.

The extra accent added by the couched yarn ties the appliques together and offers another dimension to the entire design. This vest has been comfortably worn by both men and women, so you can keep this idea in mind for a variety of people on your gift list. You'll find other couching projects in Sections 7, 16, and 28. Once you try couching and see the great effects it creates, you'll be looking for new yarn every chance you get. . . . I know, because it happened to me.

WHAT IS COUCHING?

The word *couching* has nothing to do with the piece of furniture in your living room. Instead it refers to the process of attaching one thread (usually a thicker thread, such as cord or yarn) to a backing with another thread so that only the second thread passes through the fabric. For the "Vest with Ultrasuede Squares and Yarn Couching" project, the first thread will be yarn and the second thread will be clear nylon, which will be almost invisible. Your bobbin thread should match the color of the garment or the color of the yarn, depending on the effect you're trying to create (Fig. 19-3).

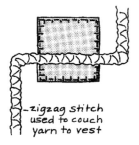

zigzag stitch used to couch yarn to vest

Figure 19-3: Yarn couched over an applique and onto the background fabric.

Yarn offers so many interesting textures on fabric. Those of us who used to knit and are still drawn to yarn can satisfy our urge to buy and use yarn by using couching to trim garments. Look for the varieties of yarn available: mohair yarns with fuzzy edges, slubbed yarns with thick and thin areas, and yarns with variegated colors all offer wonderful couching possibilities.

Many different presser feet can be used for couching. Thin yarns can be sewn in place with a cording foot. The hemmer foot, though an unconventional choice for couching, can also be used; the yarn is fed to the needle through the scroll at the front of the foot. Other presser feet you can experiment with include the lap felling foot and the zipper foot; you may have to change the needle position and use the blind hem stitch or blanket stitch. The Pearls 'N Piping specialty foot will also accommodate a thick yarn (Fig. 19-4).

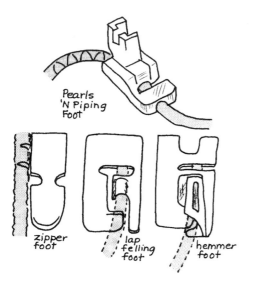

Figure 19-4: *Various presser feet can be used for couching yarn.*

The Braiding Guide attachment available from Viking sewing machine dealers is useful for couching (Fig. 19-5). The guide fits on all machines that have a hole behind the presser foot to hold a quilting guide. The Braiding Guide holds the yarn ahead of your stitching, leaving both hands free to guide the fabric. Another machine attachment, which is available for the New Home 8000, is the Miraclostitcher. This unique presser foot system couches yarn easily, again leaving both of your hands free to manipulate the fabric.

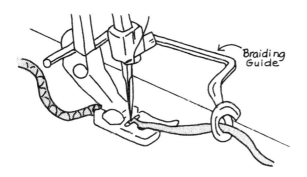

Figure 19-5: *The Braiding Guide attachment frees your hands so you can manipulate the fabric while you're couching.*

Begin sewing on the end of the yarn by back-stitching or straight stitching at 0 stitch length to secure the yarn to the base fabric (Fig. 19-6). Make sure that the yarn is free to move to the needle area and will not be caught on anything. To couch, choose a stitch that is wide enough to land on either side of the yarn. In most cases, the closer the stitching is to the edges of the yarn, the better, but don't limit yourself. Start with a narrow- to medium-width zigzag stitch and clear nylon thread. You may want the stitching to land on either side of the yarn, or you might choose to sew down the center of the yarn as you attach it to the garment. Try a variety of stitches and colors of top thread to examine their effects on the yarn and the garment. When you're finished stitching, again backstitch to attach the end of the yarn. As always, experiment and practice on scrap fabric until you feel comfortable with this technique.

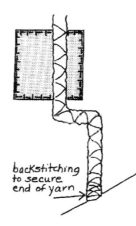

Figure 19-6: *The end of the yarn is secured by backstitching (either zigzag or straight) with the machine set to the 0 stitch length.*

Contemporary Cutwork Vest 20

Simple techniques of cutting and sewing create the unique trim on this unlined denim vest. By using modern fabrics and products, we can consider new options for traditional cutwork. For this project, you will cut holes into an unlined vest and then attach a lining behind the cutwork.

SUPPLY LIST

1 UNLINED VEST

SCRAPS OF PAPER-BACKED FUSIBLE WEB

TISSUE WRAPPING PAPER

⅔ YD. (61CM) FABRIC FOR VEST LINING

18″ (45.5CM) YARN, PEARL COTTON, OR NARROW CORDING FOR STAR TRIM

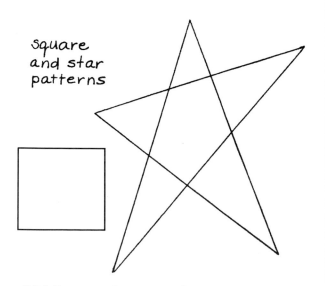

square and star patterns

Figure 20-1: Square and star cutwork patterns

1 With a water-soluble marker, trace the square pattern given in Figure 20-1 onto the right side of the vest, drawing a grouping of squares similar to that shown on the vest in the photo or planning and drawing a pattern of your choice. Leave ½″ (1.3cm) between the squares. Draw the star design given in Figure 20-1 onto the vest front near the shoulder. Trace the line continuously so that you are drawing the star the way you learned to draw stars in elementary school (Fig. 20-2).

Figure 20-2: Vest with squares and star design drawn on right side of garment.

2 I alternated between two cutting patterns—I call them "corner cuts" and "center cuts"—to cut out the squares from my vest. By cutting along different lines of the square shape, I was able to create two very different effects. Figure 20-3 shows how the two cuts are made. The corner cut squares are cut along two adjoining sides, and the center cut squares are cut diagonally from corner to corner. Before cutting into the fabric, fuse small pieces of paper-backed fusible web in the locations indicated in Figure 20-3. Remove the paper backing before cutting the squares. You'll need a pair of very sharp pointed scissors. Although they're for applique and not cutwork, pelican-billed scissors have a wonderful sharp point and are a good choice for this project (see Section 4).

Contemporary Cutwork Vest and Vest with Collar and Ties

Colorful fabrics added to plain denim vests create extra interest and detail. Lining fabric (by VIP) shows through the cutwork openings in the vest by Bagworks on the left (Section 20). Two cutwork techniques create the openings, and yarn added to the sides of the star design adds another element to the vest front. The vest on the right (by Sunbelt Sportswear) features a fabric collar and matching ties that cover the buttons and buttonholes (Section 21).

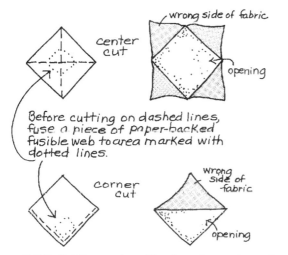

Figure 20-3: Cutting and marking lines for center cuts and corner cuts.

3 After cutting the squares, form the openings by folding back the corners of the vest fabric. Press back the corners firmly with an iron to fuse them into place.

4 To prepare the star for stitching, carefully cut away the center portion of the design (Fig. 20-4). Depending on the vest's fabric, you may want to consider Fiber Etch for this procedure (see "Cutwork Shortcut" on p.61).

Figure 20-4:
Cut away the star's center before sewing on the yarn trim.

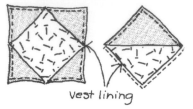

Figure 20-6: Sewing around the cutwork squares secures the cut edges of fabric and holds the lining fabric to the vest.

5 Make a pattern for the lining that will be added beneath the vest front you've treated with cutwork. Lay the vest front on top of the lining fabric so that the wrong side of the vest front faces the right side of the lining. Trace around the vest front, folding back the rest of the vest as needed to create straight edges. Add a ⅝" (1.5cm) seam allowance to all edges (Fig. 20-5). Turn the edges of the lining fabric to the *right* side and pin the lining into place on the wrong side of the vest. Make sure that the right side of the lining fabric is showing through the cutwork holes. Sew the lining to the vest front and armhole edges.

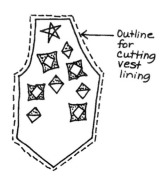

Figure 20-5:
The vest's lining pattern is created by tracing around the edges of the vest front and adding a ⅝" (1.5cm) seam allowance all around.

6 Pin the lining to the vest near the cutwork openings before sewing down the corners of the squares. Use clear or navy thread as the top thread and a bobbin thread that matches the lining fabric. The stitching will hold the fabric corners in place permanently (Fig. 20-6).

7 The star demonstrates another option for trimmed cutwork. The outline of the star is defined with yarn (or pearl cotton or narrow cording); tails of the yarn are left as fringe at four of the star's points. Use clear thread as the top thread so that the color of the yarn is not hidden. With a narrow zigzag stitch, begin sewing on the yarn at the top point of the star; sew along the line and the cut edge and down to the opposite point (Fig. 20-7). Secure the stitching and leave an extra length of yarn for fringe at the bottom point. Repeat for the other four lines of the star, leaving extra yarn at the side and bottom points of the star.

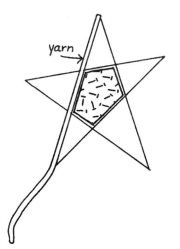

Figure 20-7:
Sew yarn along the lines of the star, leaving extra yarn at the side and bottom points as a loose fringe.

Cutwork is an easy design option that presents an interesting textural trim, which could be used on many garments. Try cutting and folding up the corners of other fabrics to see the different effects. Considering that a vest is usually worn over other clothing, you could eliminate the lining for the vest so that the cutwork openings reveal the color and fabric of the garment beneath.

CUTWORK SHORTCUT

Make use of the liquid chemical fabric remover Fiber Etch if the vest is made of cotton, rayon, or other fibrous fabric. Before attaching the vest lining and instead of sewing yarn to the outline of the star, satin stitch along the star's lines using polyester for both the top and bobbin threads. Following the manufacturer's directions, carefully apply Fiber Etch to the inside edge of the stitching outlining the center of the star. Allow the liquid to dry (you can speed up the process with a hair dryer). Iron the area and then run water over it. The fibers will have turned brown and will break, releasing the fabric in the center of the star. The satin stitch, because it is polyester, is unaffected by the chemical treatment.

Bright Idea

A trimmed vest is a great wardrobe accessory; it adds a touch of style to plain dresses and outfits. Take one along when you travel to increase the mix-and-match possibilities for a limited number of garments. By carefully planning the decorations and colors before you sew, you can create a vest that will coordinate with many outfits.

Vest with Collar & Ties 21

SUPPLY LIST

1 PLAIN VEST

TISSUE WRAPPING PAPER

³/₄ YD. (68.5CM) FABRIC FOR COLLAR AND TIES

¹/₂ YD. (46CM) LIGHTWEIGHT FUSIBLE INTERFACING

REPLACEMENT BUTTONS (OPTIONAL)

A collar added to a vest neckline frames the wearer's face and adds a decorative accent (Fig. 21-1). This project shows you how to construct a collar pattern and collar for any vest. On this vest, I also replaced very ordinary buttons with interesting ones and added tie closures made out of the collar fabric.

Figure 21-1: A floral print collar and ties add a touch of style to an ordinary denim vest.

1 Make a pattern for the collar. Fold the vest neckline in half with the back center on the fold. Place the neckline of the vest on the tissue paper. Trace the neck edge from the center back to 1¼" (3cm) from the edge of the vest fronts (Fig. 21-2). Draw a straight line along the center back fold that is 3" (7.5cm) long.

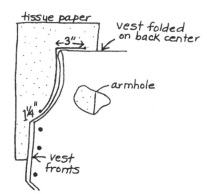

Figure 21-2: Fold the vest along the center back line and place the neck edge over tissue paper; trace the edge to make a pattern for the collar.

2 Remove the vest from the tissue paper and use the collar front curve pattern (Fig. 21-3) to draw the curved end of the collar, matching lines as indicated on the pattern. Extend the back line of the pattern to the center back drawn on the tissue, keeping 3" (7.5cm) between the two long lines. Add a ½" (1.3cm) seam allowance to the neckline edge of the collar pattern (Fig. 21-4). (You may be tempted to add a wider seam allowance, but that will make it difficult to fit the fabric collar to the curve of the vest neckline.) Cut the pattern from the tissue paper.

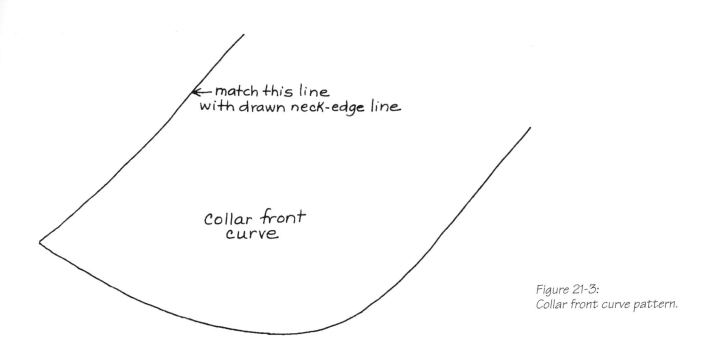

← match this line
with drawn neck-edge line

Collar front
curve

Figure 21-3:
Collar front curve pattern.

3 Fold the collar fabric in half lengthwise, right sides together, and place the center back edge of the collar pattern on the fold of the fabric. Cut two collars from fabric and one from lightweight interfacing. Fuse the light-weight interfacing to the wrong side of one of the collars to give stability, but not too much stiffness, to the completed collar. I prefer to fuse interfacing to the under collar.

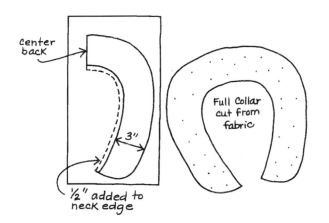

center back

Full Collar cut from fabric

3"

½" added to neck edge

Figure 21-4: Draw the collar pattern on tissue paper, adding a ½"(1.3cm) seam allowance to the neck edge of the collar pattern. To cut a whole collar, place the center back edge of the pattern on folded fabric.

4 Pin the two collar pieces together with right sides facing. Using a ¼" (6mm) seam allowance, sew along the outer edge of the collar (Fig. 21-5).

wrong side of fabric

Figure 21-5:
Sew the outer edges of the two collar pieces together, with right sides facing.

Trim and clip the seam and turn the collar right side out and press. Zigzag or serge the raw edges of the collar together (Fig. 21-6). Your collar is now ready to be attached to the vest.

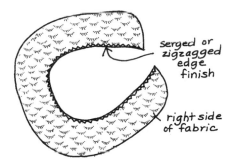

serged or zigzagged edge finish

right side of fabric

Figure 21-6: The collar is now ready to be attached to the vest.

5 Position the center back of the collar's serged or zigzagged inner edge so that it just overlaps the back neck edge of the vest, with the under collar facing the wrong side of the vest. Pin the collar to the vest, starting from the collar's center point. Check the collar ends to see that they are lined up evenly when the vest is buttoned (Fig. 21-7).

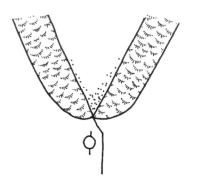

Figure 21-7: Make sure that the ends of the collar meet evenly when the vest is closed.

Once the collar is pinned in place, sew on top of the serging or zigzagging to attach the collar to the vest (Fig. 21-8). The seam allowance should be very small. Press the collar and the vest neckline after stitching.

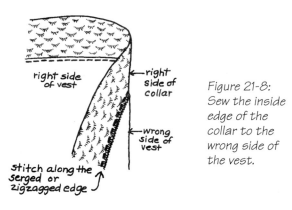

Figure 21-8: Sew the inside edge of the collar to the wrong side of the vest.

6 The next step is to replace the buttons on the vest. You can select buttons from your collection or purchase new ones. Changing the buttons will usually be a big improvement to the vest or will at least make it more interesting.

7 To make the two sets of ties, cut a piece of fabric 24 x 2" (61 x 5cm). Fold the fabric strip in half along the 2" (5cm) edge, right sides together (Fig. 21-9).

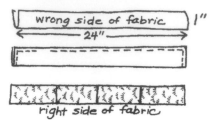

Figure 21-9: Fold the fabric strip in half and sew along the raw edges, leaving a gap for turning.

Sew the raw edges of the fabric together with a ¼" (6mm) seam allowance, leaving an opening for turning. Pull the fabric through the opening, turning the fabric strip right side out; press the strip. (For a quick way to turn the fabric right side out, try Fasturn tubes [available at sewing stores].) Cut the strip into four equal pieces. On each tube, turn the raw ends to the inside of the tube and sew or fuse them in place. Sew the ends of the finished tube to each side of the vest front (Fig. 21-10); the ties will fold over the stitching, hiding both the buttons and buttonholes, when tied.

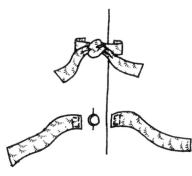

Figure 21-10: Sew the ties on either side of the buttons and buttonholes.

Though the collar on my vest was left plain, think of the ways you could spark it up—with decorative stitching, appliques, or other trims—to add an extra element of detail to your vest.

Vest with Ribbon Trim 22

A collection of unique ribbons works as great trim for the simple vest on page 66. While many vests are trimmed with fabrics and laces in a horizontal pattern, I chose to work with a vertical design.

SUPPLY LIST

1 PLAIN VEST

1/4 YD. (23CM) OR 1 ROLL OF PAPER-BACKED FUSIBLE WEB

A SELECTION OF RIBBONS, EACH AT LEAST 18" (46CM) LONG (USE WASHABLE RIBBONS IF YOU INTEND TO WASH THE VEST.)

1/2 YD. (46CM) TEAR-AWAY STABILIZER (OPTIONAL)

3 YD. (2.75M) OF BIAS TAPE TO MATCH THE VEST

ULTRASUEDE SCRAPS FOR BUTTON LOOPS

PAPER FOR BUTTON LOOP TEMPLATE

3 BUTTONS FOR NEW VEST CLOSURE

1 If your vest has buttons, remove them first. Then plan the layout of ribbons on the vest fronts, referring to the vest in the photo or using your own design. The ribbons should butt up against each other so that the vest is not visible through the ribbon covering. If you line up your ribbons vertically, as I did, the ribbons at the neck and armhole edge will extend past the edge (Fig. 22-1). This is not a problem, because these ribbon ends will be cut off later. At the shoulder edge of the vest, it is important that the ribbons extend beyond the edge; these ends will be turned under later. Cut the bottom ends of the ribbons at an angle, as I did, or cut them straight. These edges can be turned under or treated with Fray Check. Once you have decided on the layout of your cut ribbons, trace the outline of the bottom edges of the ribbons with washable marker on the vest front. (Use marker only if your decorated vest is going to be washable; if not, use pins to mark the ribbon placement.) You may also want to number your ribbons, using Post-it Notes, so that you remember which ribbon goes where.

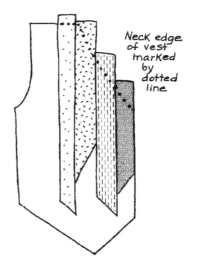

Figure 22-1: Plan the ribbon layout so that there is extra length at neckline and shoulder edges.

Neck edge of vest marked by dotted line

2 Fuse narrow strips of paper-backed fusible web to the wrong sides of the ribbons along the long edges (Fig. 22-2). The strips can be cut from yardage (done quickly with the rotary cutter, ruler, and mat) or cut from a narrow roll to save time. If the fusible web were applied to the entire ribbon, the vest front would be too stiff.

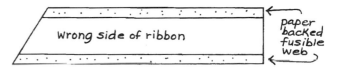

Wrong side of ribbon

paper backed fusible web

Figure 22-2: Narrow strips of paper-backed fusible web are fused to the ribbons' edges.

Vest with Ribbon Trim

It's easy to see how a variety of ribbons can turn a plain vest into a garment with style. Vertical strips of ribbons by Offray are sewn to an unlined vest by Bagworks. Closures of Ultrasuede and unusual buttons complete the new look for the garment.

3   Remove the paper backing from the strips of web and fuse the ribbons to the vest, beginning at the center front edge of the vest (Fig. 22-3). (You should complete the fusing and sewing on one side of the vest before working on the other side.) Follow the layout lines you drew in Step 1, and remember to butt the ribbons up against one another. Do not fuse the top of the ribbons that reach the vest's shoulder seam; instead, turn these top edges to the wrong side of the ribbon and line up the fold of the ribbon with the shoulder seam.

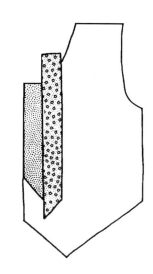

Figure 22-3: Fuse the ribbons to vest beginning at the center front edge.

4 If your vest is made of a soft fabric, you may need to pin or attach stabilizer to the wrong side of the vest fronts before sewing on the ribbons; this will give you a sturdier sewing surface. Use clear nylon thread as the top thread and match the bobbin thread to the vest. Adjust your machine to a medium-width zigzag stitch and sew over the butted edges of two ribbons so that the zigzag catches both ribbons. Sew across the bottom edge of one of the ribbons and up the side of the next two butted ribbons (Fig. 22-4). Continue this procedure until all of the ribbons are attached to this side of the vest front. Next, use a zigzag stitch to scw along the shoulder seam to attach the folded-under top edges of the ribbons to the vest.

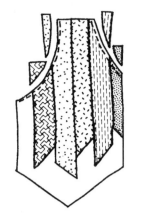

Figure 22-5: After stitching over the ribbons at the armholes and front neck edge, trim away the excess ribbon.

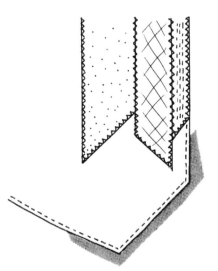

Figure 22-4: Zigzag stitch with clear thread along the sides and bottom edges of the ribbons.

5 Follow Steps 3 and 4 to cover the other side of the vest.

6 At the armholes and front neck edges, secure the ends of the ribbons by straight stitching close to the edge of the vest. After stitching, trim off any ribbon that extends beyond these edges (Fig. 22-5).

7 Use bias tape (purchased or made) to finish the armhole and neck edges of the vest. Sew the right side of the bias tape to the right side of the vest, along the tape's fold, and then flip the tape over the vest edges and sew it down to the back side of the vest. Or, wrap the tape over the edges and topstitch through all layers (Fig. 22-6).

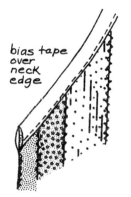

bias tape over neck edge

Figure 22-6: Wrap and sew bias tape over the neck edge and armholes of the vest.

8 Now it's time to add a new closure to the vest front. The vest in the photo has three ribbon loops that wrap around a new set of buttons. Create one ribbon loop for each of the now-covered buttonholes on your vest, or choose the number of loops that you think looks good. Trace the button-loop pattern from Figure 22-7 onto a piece of paper and cut out the shape. Trace and cut out several paper ribbon loops if you want to see how more than one will look on your vest. As you plan your closure, decide on the buttons you'll use with the ribbon loops.

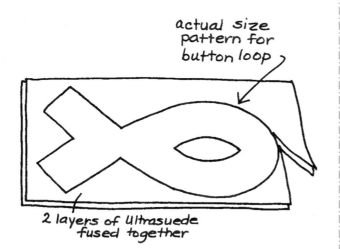

actual size pattern for button loop

2 layers of Ultrasuede fused together

Figure 22-7: The button loop is cut from two layers of Ultrasuede that have been fused together.

9 The following directions are for three ribbon loops; adjust the instructions for the number of loops you plan to add to your vest. Fuse three 1½" x 3" (4 x 7.5cm) pieces of paper-backed fusible web to the wrong side of pieces of Ultrasuede and cut out the rectangles. Remove the paper backing and fuse each rectangle to the wrong side of a matching size piece of Ultrasuede; use a press cloth to protect the surface of the suede fabric. Use the paper template you made in Step 8 to trace the button-loop shape onto each double-layered Ultrasuede rectangle; cut out the shapes (Fig. 22-7). Adjust the size of the center opening to fit the buttons you've chosen for your vest.

10 Position and pin the buttonhole loops to the right front of the vest. Using the photo as a guide, topstitch along the edges of the portion of the loop that is on the vest. Sew buttons onto the other vest front, and you're ready to wear your latest creation.

Enjoy shopping for ribbons for this project or searching through your collection.

Jewelry-Inspired Vest 23

A man's suit vest, hanging unused in the closet, finds a new life with appliques inspired by the necklace shown in the photo on page 70. The shapes of the rubber necklace are repeated, in larger form, in a vine pattern on the vest. Study your jewelry box; you may find a special piece that could inspire a project.

SUPPLY LIST

1 PLAIN VEST

ULTRASUEDE (OR OTHER FABRIC) IN JEWELRY COLORS

1/4 YD. (23CM) PAPER-BACKED FUSIBLE WEB

1/4 YD. (23CM) TEAR-AWAY STABILIZER

1 The first step in this project is selecting the jewelry piece to duplicate on your vest. The pattern for the design I used is given in Figure 23-1, but I hope you'll consider recreating a jewelry design of your own. It's not necessary to use the exact size or even the colors of the jewelry you want to copy; in fact, you may want to enlarge the shapes, as I did. Trace the actual earring, necklace, pin, or bracelet motif on paper. Enlarge the tracing on a copy machine or free hand. Will a repetition of the shape look good on your vest? Or maybe the motif should be enlarged so that only one shape will fit on your vest? Considering these options (as well as choosing the piece of jewelry to use for your design) is part of the overall design process, which gives you a chance to be truly creative. "Design Decisions," in this section, provides hints and helpful information to guide you through that process.

2 It makes good sense to plan a design arrangement on a garment with paper copies of the design shapes. Rather than cut many shapes from Ultrasuede and later discard them because you want to change the design or color scheme, use colored paper for the shapes. Cut the shapes from Ultrasuede only after you've made a final decision about the designs, number of motifs, and their colors (see "Design Decisions" for more information). You'll also want to have paper-backed fusible web on the wrong side of the fabric. For my vest, I traced the shapes onto paper-backed fusible web, cut them out, fused them to the wrong side of colored scraps of Ultrasuede (using the necklace colors as a guide), and then cut the shapes from the Ultrasuede. I then removed the paper backing and fused the shapes to the vest before sewing.

alternative applique design

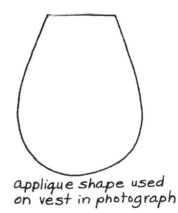

applique shape used on vest in photograph

Figure 23-1: Jewelry shapes to use for applique

Jewelry-Inspired Vest

Use the shapes of jewelry, like those in the necklace shown here, to create appliques to sew to a vest. The appliques are cut from Ultrasuede and sewn onto a man's suit vest with clear nylon thread.

3 Stabilizer is an important addition to the vest prior to sewing. Pin or attach a piece in place on the wrong side of the vest beneath the areas that are to be decorated.

4 Choose a thread color and stitch for attaching the appliques to the vest (see "Design Decisions"), and stitch around them. If you are using a fraying fabric for the appliques (and you don't want frayed edges to be part of the design), choose a satin or other dense stitch.

5 After the sewing is complete, remove the stabilizer from the back of the vest.

Combining your appliqued vest with the piece of jewelry that inspired it will result in a designer wearable that cannot be found in stores. Once again, your sewing and designing skills give you the ability to create something unique and individual that no one else owns.

DESIGN DECISIONS

It takes time to plan successful decorations for any garment. You may be eager to get to the fun part of sewing the design in place, but the time you spend making decisions about your design will be important in the creation of a stylish and professionally decorated garment. Here are my suggestions to help you make choices when trimming clothing.

The first step, always, is to try on the garment and to mark the bustline points with pins or a water soluble marker. The two marks will help you to avoid placing prominent design shapes directly on the bustline.

One way I work with shapes and plan designs is to cut the shapes from paper, sometimes colored paper if color is one of the choices I'm making. Cutting from paper is an easy and economical way to test both the size and color of an applique or other design before cutting it from fabric. There's no limit to how you can position the paper shapes and pin them on the garment. Rather than place the shapes in a traditional or expected way, be bold and pin them upside down, sideways, or overlapping one another. You may discover that an unusual placement of your chosen design will give an artistic touch to the garment.

Study your proposed design from a distance; squint at it to see if you like the way the design colors interact with the garment color (Fig. 23-2). Try the garment on again to check the size, color, and placement of the shapes. Look at the garment in a mirror. Ask for an opinion from someone else. You're likely to get honest critiques from children and adults who live with you. They don't have to be skilled at sewing to be able to offer responses that will help you determine whether your ideas are good. If a person takes a long time to respond or she appears to hesitate and not know what to say, this may be a sign that your planned design is not yet as attractive or effective as you would like. My experience has taught me that an immediate positive response is the best indication that I've got a design plan worth keeping.

Figure 23-2: Study a design idea from a distance to get a different perspective on color and design placement.

Once you've got a design plan, trace around the edges or corners of the paper shapes with a washable marker to mark their placement. This will help you recreate the design with fabrics exactly as you planned it with paper patterns.

Choosing the color, shapes, and placement of an applique design is important, but it's not the "whole picture." The overall look of your decorated garment will also be affected by how you stitch the shapes to the garment. The type and color of thread, as well as the stitch itself, can become part of the design. If you want the stitching to be a noticeable addition to the design, use a contrasting color of thread and a decorative stitch. I often prefer to use clear nylon thread as the top thread and a color matching the garment for the bobbin thread. Thread that matches the applique fabric is another option for stitching that blends in with the design. A narrow zigzag, blindhem, or blanket stitch would be a good choice if you want a hidden, unnoticeable seam attaching the appliques to the garment. Satin stitching, which has the added benefit of preventing the applique fabric from fraying, can be used as a blending or contrasting element, depending on the thread color you choose.

There are so many choices to make before you sew the first stitch. When you take time to study the garment, along with the fabric, thread, and design layout possibilities, you will have a better chance of turning out a garment that has style and your own designer's touch.

Shirts
Part Five

Cavalry Bib Shirt

24

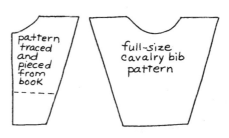

Figure 24-1: Construct a full-size bib pattern and test the size and shape on the front of your shirt.

Though *bib* is a word associated with babies, it also describes the shirt front decoration shown in the photo on page 74. Styled after the shirts worn by soldiers, the bib front brings a new look to a shirt and offers endless trimming options.

SUPPLY LIST

1 PLAIN BUTTON-FRONT SHIRT

TISSUE WRAPPING PAPER OR PATTERN TRACING PAPER

½ YD. (46CM) BIB FABRIC OR ½ YD. (46CM) EACH OF TWO DIFFERENT FABRICS FOR REVERSIBLE BIB

ONE 14 X 16″(35.5 X 40.5CM) PIECE OF LIGHTWEIGHT FUSIBLE INTERFACING

12 BUTTONS

1 The bib pattern is shown in Figure 24-3 (p. 75). Trace the two sections of the pattern onto tissue paper or pattern tracing paper, connecting them on the lines indicated. Align the edge of the pieced pattern with a fold in the tissue paper, where indicated, to make the complete bib pattern (Fig. 24-1). Cut out the pattern and test its size.

2 Try on the shirt to which you will attach the bib and pin the bib pattern to the shirt front. Remember that ¼″ (6mm) seam allowances are included on the pattern. If the pattern is too large or too small or needs any other adjustment, change the pattern now.

3 Trace and cut out two bibs from fabric (one for the bib front and one for the bib back) and one bib from interfacing. The bib will be reversible, as shown in the photo, if you use different fabrics for the front and back. Fuse the interfacing to the wrong side of one of the fabric bibs.

4 Pin the fabrics with right sides together and sew around the edges, leaving a 2″ (5cm) opening on one side of the bib (Fig. 24-2). Trim and clip into the seam allowances and turn the bib right side out. Press the bib flat and close the seam opening with hand stitching, if you think it needs to be closed. I like Sue Hausmann's idea: she's saving all of these seam openings to sew in her retirement.

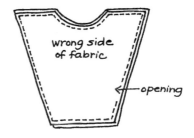

Figure 24-2: Sew the two bib pieces together, leaving an opening to turn the bib right side out.

Cavalry Bib Shirt

Make a variety of bibs to interchange on a shirt front. The bib buttoned to the shirt is made from Ultrasuede. Shapes cut using both straight and circular buttonhole cutters decorate the bib. The second bib, shown with one corner folded back, is made of two cotton fabrics so that it can be reversible.

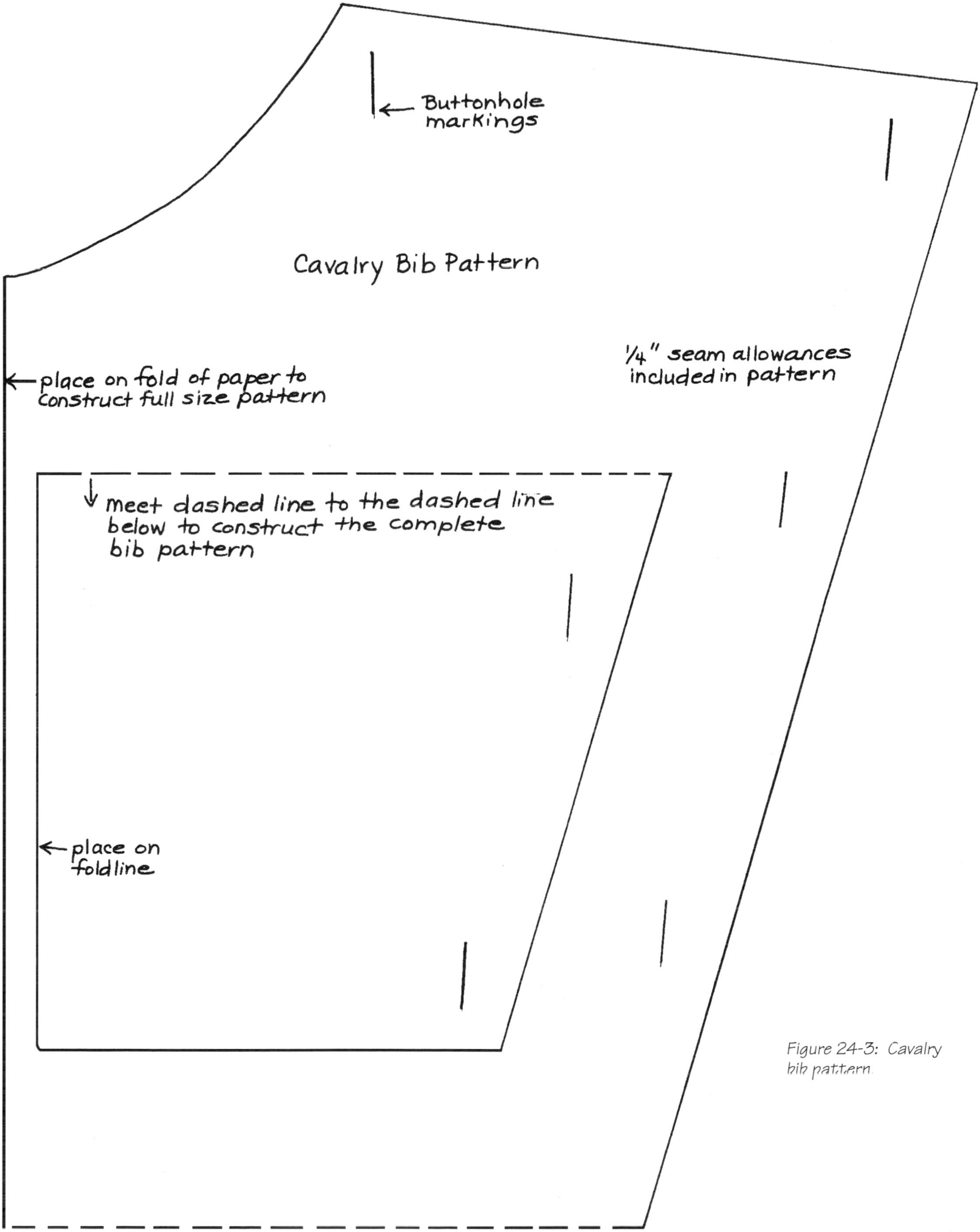

Buttonhole
markings

Cavalry Bib Pattern

¼" seam allowances
included in pattern

place on fold of paper to
construct full size pattern

meet dashed line to the dashed line
below to construct the complete
bib pattern

place on
foldline

Figure 24-3: Cavalry
bib pattern

5 The next task is to sew the buttonholes in the bib. With a chalk marker, mark the locations of the buttonholes along either the right or left edge of the bib, following the pattern (Fig. 24-3). An easy way to mark the buttonholes on the other edge of the bib is to fold the bib in half and rub over the buttonhole markings so that the chalk marks are transferred to the other side of the bib front (Fig. 24-4). This guarantees that the buttonholes will be made in the same locations on each side, which is especially important if the bib will be reversible.

Figure 24-4: Draw buttonhole markings on one side of bib with chalk marker, fold the bib in half, and rub the bib carefully along the markings to transfer them to the other side of the bib.

6 Choose the thread colors carefully for the buttonholes, especially if the bib is to be reversible. Decide on the buttons you want to use on the shirt, and then sew the appropriate buttonholes into the bib. Many newer sewing machines have built-in, automatic buttonhole options, which will help you breeze through this part of the project. Cut open the buttonholes after stitching them.

7 Lay the bib flat on the shirt front and pin it into place around the edges. Insert the tip of a fabric marker through the center of each buttonhole to mark the location of the buttons that will be sewn to the shirt (Fig. 24-5). If you have chosen flat buttons with holes through the centers, you'll be able to sew the buttons on by machine. Shank buttons must be sewn on by hand. Or, pin shank buttons into place with small gold metallic safety pins (I call this the metallic method) so that you can switch buttons or wear the shirt plain.

Figure 24-5: Mark the button locations through the buttonhole openings.

The pink Ultrasuede bib in the photo is an easy no-sew option. The Ultrasuede was cut with a wavy-edge rotary cutter, and the buttonholes were made with a buttonhole cutter. To add further interest, consider cutting designs out of the Ultrasuede so the shirt color shows through the holes. I have used a buttonhole cutter, straightedge cutter, and a keyhole cutter (which makes the small circles) to create this type of detail.

By now you may be thinking about lots of other possibilities for the cavalry bib . . . an appliqued or patchwork front, a lace-trimmed or corded-edge front, or a showcase for decorative stitching done by hand or with your sewing machine. With one shirt and a variety of cavalry bibs, your wardrobe will expand.

Pillow-Panel Trimmed Shirts

25

SUPPLY LIST

1 TUXEDO SHIRT

1 PILLOW PANEL WITH ACCOMPANYING BORDER FABRICS

¹/₄ YD. (23CM) PAPER-BACKED FUSIBLE WEB

W hen you study a pillow panel (or "cheater quilt block," as quilters call them), you'll realize that there are many areas and parts that can be used to trim garments. Usually you buy two panels on ½ yd. (46cm) of fabric, which will give you many options for cutting up and using the prints. See Figure 25-9 for additional ideas.

Tuxedo Shirt with Pillow Panel

On the tuxedo shirt in the photo on page 78, the front trim was cut from the center floral area of the panel; the top corner of the square was cut off to raise the panel on the body of the shirt (Fig. 25-1). On larger shirts, more of the decorative panel area can be used.

1 With the shirt buttoned, decide on the size and diagonal placement of the pillow panel on the shirt. Plan for a seam allowance of at least ¼" (6mm) on all four edges of the square. Cut out the square with extra fabric for seam allowances. Turn under and press the seam allowances to the back of the panel along all four edges.

2 Test the panel on the shirt front again. Does it extend over the armhole seam line? You may want to make the square smaller, which you'll do after cutting the square in half. If the panel size does not need to be altered, fold the square in half along the diagonal, unfold the square, and fuse a ½"-wide (1.3cm) strip of paper-backed fusible web to the wrong side of the fabric, centering it on the diagonal fold line. Then cut the square in half along the diagonal line, and you'll have a ¼" (6mm) strip of fusing material on each half of the panel's center edges. If the panel needs to be smaller, fold the square in half along the diagonal, and cut the square in half along this fold. Carefully trim away fabric along each side of the diagonal fold line until the panel fits your shirt (Fig. 25-2).

Figure 25-1: Pillow panel square placement on tuxedo shirt

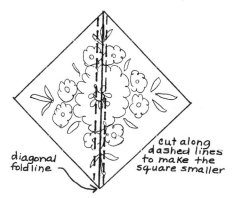

Figure 25-2: Make the panel smaller by cutting fabric from the center, along the diagonal fold line.

Pillow-Panel Yoke Shirt and Tuxedo Shirt with Pillow Panel

Plain white shirts get stylish with portions of pillow panel fabrics added. A pillow panel (by VIP Fabrics) is positioned as a yoke section on the top shirt, with additional areas of the panel used for the cuffs and pocket trim. The middle section of a pillow square is centered diagonally on the tuxedo shirt (bottom garment) and the cuffs are covered with the border section from the same panel.

Fuse a ¼" (6mm) strip of paper-backed fusible web to the wrong side of the long edge of each half of the altered pillow panel (Fig. 25-3).

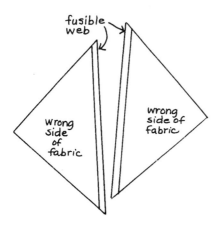

Figure 25-3: Strips of paper-backed fusible web are applied to the wrong side of the long edges of each half of the panel.

3 With the shirt still buttoned, place the long edge of each half of the square just under the edge of the shirt placket. These cut edges of the panel will be hidden beneath the folded placket edges, and, since they are cut on the bias, they will not ravel. Before fusing these long cut edges in place along the placket sides, trim the top point of each panel half to match the curve of the shirt's neck band and turn the raw edge under (Fig. 25-4). Clip into the seam allowance if necessary to get the fabric to cooperate as you turn it under. After these points are clipped, remove the paper backing from each half of the panel and fuse each half along one edge of the shirt's placket.

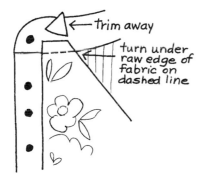

Figure 25-4: Cut off excess fabric and turn under the edge of the panel where the fabric meets the neck band of the shirt.

4 Next, pin the outside edges of the panel to the shirt; topstitch along all three edges of each panel half to attach the pillow panel to the garment. On the outside edges, I enhanced the straight stitching with a decorative machine stitch that extended from the panel fabric onto the shirt (Fig. 25-5). This extra trim is optional.

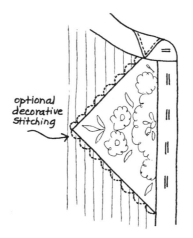

Figure 25-5: The optional decorative machine stitching adds edge detail to the sides of the panel.

5 Covering the shirt cuffs makes sense both as an extension of the shirt's decoration and also to cover an area that is a challenge to keep clean. I used two different sections of the panel to cover the cuffs. Note that I broke with tradition: Who says that both cuffs have to look the same?

6 Cut a piece of fabric larger all around than the shirt's cuff. Turn under and press one long edge of the fabric piece, and then pin this folded edge to the sleeve seam of the cuff. The wrong side of the fabric piece should face the right side of the cuff, and the fabric piece should cover the cuff.

7 You can cover the cuff without removing the button with this procedure: On the wrong side of the cover fabric, fuse a ½" (1.3cm) square piece of paper-backed fusible web (make it larger if the shirt's cuff button is large) on the spot where the button touches the fabric. Peel off the paper backing and make a small straight cut in the cover fabric, just large enough to get the button through (Fig. 25-6). Slip the button through the slit, and immediately fuse the cover fabric around the button.

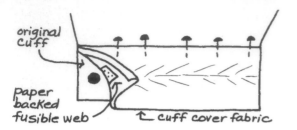

original cuff

paper backed fusible web

cuff cover fabric

Figure 25-6: Fuse a piece of paper-backed fusible web to the wrong side of the cuff cover fabric, remove the paper backing, cut a slit just large enough to get the button through, and fuse the edges of the opening around the button. With this method, you don't have to remove the button.

8 Now turn under, press, and pin the other raw edges of the cuff cover to the edges of the cuff. Sew around the cover to attach it to the shirt. Match the bobbin thread to the shirt color for a less noticeable seam. (If you roll up your sleeves, the back side of the stitching will show.)

9 To reopen the buttonholes in the cuffs, sew a narrow zigzag stitch around the buttonholes on the wrong side of the cuffs. Cut the button-holes open (Fig. 25-7). If your tuxedo shirt has two buttonholes on each cuff and you plan to wear cuff links, make sure to stitch and then cut open both sets of buttonholes.

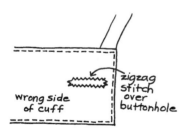

wrong side of cuff

zigzag stitch over buttonhole

Figure 25-7: Sew a narrow zigzag around the buttonhole on the wrong side of the cuff. Then cut open the buttonhole through the cuff cover fabric.

You'll have leftover scraps of the pillow panel fabrics and if you don't want to stop decorating the tuxedo shirt, consider adding fabric to the collar, or making a bow tie out of the extra fabric. Your classy tuxedo shirt just got classier with help from a pillow panel.

Pillow-Panel Yoke Shirt

Select a pillow panel to create interesting trim for a plain white shirt. On the shirt shown on page 78, only one side of the shirt was covered, though both sides could be trimmed and the pocket eliminated. The panel yoke creates an extra layer, similar to the flap on a trench coat. Other portions of the pillow panel fabric were used to trim other parts of the shirt.

SUPPLY LIST

1 WHITE BUTTON-FRONT SHIRT

1 PILLOW PANEL WITH ACCOMPANYING BORDER FABRICS

TISSUE WRAPPING PAPER

FUSIBLE WEB (OPTIONAL)

NEW BUTTONS FOR SHIRT (OPTIONAL)

1 Pin-trace a yoke pattern, following the directions in Section 6. Figure 25-8 shows the dimensions of the yoke.

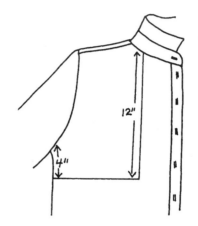

12"

4"

Figure 25-8: Dimensions of the yoke.

If you want to change the length or width of the yoke, adjust your paper pattern accordingly. Cut the pattern from the corner of the pillow panel design, leaving extra fabric on all sides of the pattern as shown in Figure 25-9.

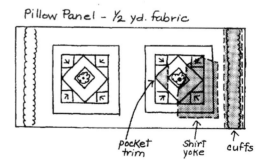

Pillow Panel - ½ yd. fabric

pocket trim

shirt yoke

cuffs

Figure 25-9: Gray areas indicate where to cut the shirt trim from the pillow panel fabric.

2 Then press under and sew or fuse back the straight side and bottom edge of the yoke (Fig. 25-10).

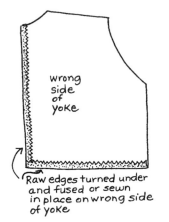

wrong side of yoke

Raw edges turned under and fused or sewn in place on wrong side of yoke

Figure 25-10: The side and bottom edge of the yoke are turned to the wrong side of the fabric and stitched or fused in place.

3 Pin the panel to the shirt along the panel's straight side and bottom edge, making sure there is excess fabric to turn back at the other edges. Turn under and pin the remaining edges, lining up the folds of the fabric to the seam lines on the shirt's arm, shoulder, and neck. If the panel fabric is difficult to fold under in a curve, clip into the seam allowances. Topstitch the panel to the shirt, sewing close to the edges you just turned under. To keep the panel lying in place and flat on the shirt front, sew along the long straight side and the bottom edge of the design approximately 1½" (4cm) in from the outer edges (Fig. 25-11), following one of the lines in the design pattern.

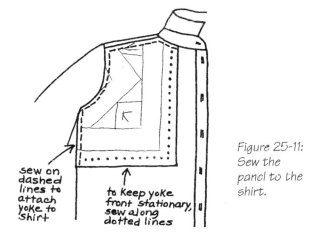

sew on dashed lines to attach yoke to shirt

to keep yoke front stationary, sew along dotted lines

Figure 25-11: Sew the panel to the shirt.

4 Plan the other decorative additions to the shirt. Other areas to trim include the collar, cuffs, pocket, and shirt back. I originally planned to cover the collar on my shirt, but I decided that the embroidery on the collar coordinated well with the panel so I left it alone. (Sometimes you get lucky with the garment's own details.) To trim the shirt pocket, first try on the shirt to determine if the pocket's location is right for

you. On my shirt, I decided that the pocket was too low, so I removed it and added trim from another corner of the pillow panel before reattaching it to the shirt. As with the front panel, I turned under the edges of the pocket trim and topstitched it to the pocket. Hint: Use a clear nylon thread as the top thread when sewing on a multicolored fabric so that the thread will blend in with all the colors. Use regular sewing thread in the bobbin, because nylon thread could irritate your skin.

5 The cuffs were covered with the strip of coordinating border fabric near the selvedge edge of the panel fabric (see Fig. 25-9). The fabric cover was cut larger than the actual shirt cuff by at least ½" (1.3cm) on all sides. Turn under, press, and pin one long edge to the upper edge of the shirt's cuff.

6 Remove the cuff button or buttons or leave them on the shirt. If you decide to leave them on, use the method described in Step 7 for the "Tuxedo Shirt with Pillow Panel" earlier in this section.

7 Next, follow Steps 8 and 9 of the "Tuxedo Shirt with Pillow Panel" earlier in this section. At the bottom edge of the cuff, you can either turn under the fabric, as you did on the other edges, or wrap the excess fabric to the inside of the sleeve. This method hides any stains or signs of wear and might give the shirt a longer life (Fig 25-12).

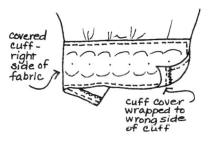

covered cuff - right side of fabric

cuff cover wrapped to wrong side of cuff

Figure 25-12: Fold the cuff cover fabric around the bottom edge of the cuff edge to cover signs of wear.

8 To complete the shirt's renovation, change the buttons to coordinate with the panel colors.

Ever since pillow panel fabrics became available at fabric shops, I have been attracted to them and couldn't resist buying them (I have many of them!). If you have a similar stash of these fabrics, consider using them to trim your clothing.

Patchwork Shirt with Placket Cover

26

Use a collection of fabric swatches from your own stash or exchange with a friend for this collage of colored pieces. You could also use an assortment of fabric swatches acquired through a mail-order fabric club (check listings in sewing magazines). Trim the pinked edges, and check the washability of the swatches you select. I chose a collection of fabrics from applique and quilting projects from the 1970s and 1980s for the shirt shown on page 84. Have you noticed how cotton prints change through the years? The prints available in stores now are quite different from the ones we bought even five years ago. The other additions to the shirt are covers for the collar and the placket.

SUPPLY LIST

1 PLAIN BUTTON-FRONT SHIRT, WITH POCKETS REMOVED

COLLECTION OF FABRIC SWATCHES

¼ YD. (23CM) PAPER-BACKED FUSIBLE WEB

¼ YD. (23CM) STABILIZER

TISSUE WRAPPING PAPER

¼ YD. (23CM) FABRIC FOR COLLAR COVER

½ YD. (46CM) FABRIC FOR PLACKET COVER

1/4 YD. (23CM) LIGHTWEIGHT FUSIBLE INTERFACING (OPTIONAL)

1–3 BUTTONS (OPTIONAL)

VELCRO (OPTIONAL)

1 After applying paper-backed fusible web to the wrong side of the fabric swatches, remove the paper backing and arrange the swatches on one side of the shirt's front. Use the design on my shirt for a guide or plan your own arrangement. (I'm never upset if you tell me that you haven't used my designs exactly as I show them. I'm glad if my designs inspire you to create your own pattern. That's your personal touch, which makes your work individual and unique.) Once the arrangement looks good to you, fuse the swatches in place. Add stabilizer to the wrong side of the shirt front, and get ready to sew.

2 You'll notice that I used black thread (Sulky rayon) and a variety of decorative machine stitches to sew the edges of the swatches (Fig. 26-1). Experiment with the stitches on scrap fabrics with stabilizer beneath. To make sure the bobbin thread does not show, decrease the top tension or match the bobbin thread to the top thread. This might be a good project for using as many decorative machine stitches as you can.

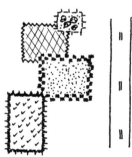

Figure 26-1: The fabric patches are attached with decorative stitches using black rayon thread.

3 Once the patchwork swatches are in place, select a coordinating fabric to cover the collar. Pin-trace the shirt's collar to make a pattern, following the instructions in Section 6. Cut the pattern from the fabric, leaving a seam allowance all around. Turn under and pin the long straight edge of the fabric to meet the collar stand of the shirt (Fig. 26-2).

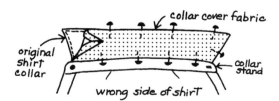

Figure 26-2: Pin and sew on a new cover for the collar.

Turn under and pin the other three edges to line up with the edges of the original collar. Topstitch the collar cover to the shirt's collar.

4 Make a placket cover pattern from the diagram in Figure 26-3. Hold the paper pattern up to measure its fit on your body and/or the shirt you're working on. Note that the pattern can be shortened or lengthened at the bottom end.

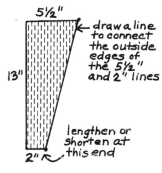

Figure 26-3: Placket cover pattern.

5 Cut two placket cover pieces from the fabric, noting the grain line. If the fabrics you chose are soft or thin, you'll probably need to apply lightweight fusible interfacing to the wrong side of one of the cover pieces. Pin the two cover pieces together, right sides facing, and sew with a ¼" (6mm) seam allowance along the three edges indicated in Figure 26-4. Trim the seam allowance and corners with pinking shears, turn right sides of the fabric out, and press.

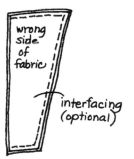

Figure 26-4: With right sides of the fabric together, sew around three sides of the placket cover.

6 With the right side of the placket cover facing the shirt front, place and pin the raw edges of the cover at the edge of the original shirt placket. Sew this edge of the cover to the shirt, using a ¼" (6mm) seam allowance (Fig. 26-5). Turn the placket cover over the shirt placket and press the folded edge. Sew a buttonhole in the outside corner of the placket cover (Fig. 26-6). You might want to add another button and buttonhole or Velcro to keep the placket cover flat on the shirt while it is worn.

Figure 26-5: Sew the placket cover to the buttonhole side of the shirt front.

7 Sew a button to the shirt to hold the placket. Or, as I did, sew a tie to the shirt that can be pulled through the buttonhole and knotted. Refer to Figure 26-7 and Step 7 in Section 21 for instructions on making ties. Once the tie or button is affixed, try on the shirt and check that the bottom and lower side of the placket cover lie flat.

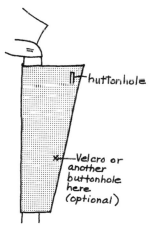

Figure 26-6: Add a buttonhole to the upper corner of the placket cover. Add another buttonhole (or Velcro), if desired.

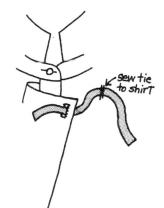

Figure 26-7: Sew a ribbon or tie to the shirt front instead of a button; pull both ends of the tie through the buttonhole and knot them to keep the placket closed. (I used two different fabrics to create my tie.)

Patchwork Shirt with Placket Cover

A collection of fabric patches with decorative machine stitching on them trims one side of a white shirt. The very ordinary collar and placket are covered with additional fabric, and the placket cover is held in place with ties sewn to the shirt and knotted through a buttonhole in the placket cover.

8 Because most plain white shirts have such ordinary buttons, I suggest that you replace the top button on the shirt—the one on the collar stand—with a more interesting one. The other boring buttons are hidden behind the placket cover.

Think about all the options you have with the placket cover and how it could be trimmed with stitching, applique, pucker stitching (see the Sunflower Apron in Section 40), or your own invention. The collar could also be treated with decorations or completely replaced by removing the original collar and making a new one in its place. It's really not difficult, since the old collar is there for you to copy. For another patchwork idea, see the Patchwork Sweater in Section 35.

Western-Style Trimmed Shirts 27

Now that country western music is in style, so are the fashions that go with it. Here are just two ideas for button-front shirts with a western flair. Use your imagination to take other ideas in this book back to the Old West. Sometimes an addition as simple as fringe or silver buttons can change the entire feel of a garment.

Bandanna-Trimmed Shirt

Ordinary bandannas add a fresh touch and a western accent to a chambray shirt. On page 86, you see them used to create two front panels, shoulder covers, and cuffs. They could also cover the collar or the front shirt placket.

SUPPLY LIST

1 PLAIN BUTTON-FRONT SHIRT

TISSUE WRAPPING PAPER

½ YD. (46CM) LIGHTWEIGHT FUSIBLE INTERFACING (I PREFER TRICOT KNIT)

ONE 22" (56CM) BANDANNA (PREWASHED) FOR FRONT PANELS

ONE 18" (46CM) BANDANNA (PREWASHED) FOR SHOULDER COVERS AND CUFFS

OTHER WESTERN TRIM, SUCH AS SILVER COLLAR POINTS, DECORATIVE BUTTONS, AND PLACKET DECORATION

1 Prepare the shirt for the trim by removing the front pockets, if they will be in the way of the front panels. After you have removed the stitching that held on the pockets, press the shirt from the wrong side first and then the right side to flatten and smooth the shirt fronts. Don't worry about marks left on the shirt from the pockets as they will be covered by the bandanna panels.

2 Make patterns for both sides of the shirt front using the pin-tracing method (see Section 6). Figure 27-1 shows the dimensions of the bandanna panels. Cut each pattern piece from the fusible interfacing.

Figure 27-1: Panel dimensions for shirt front.

3 Place the panel patterns on the corners of the larger bandanna. Don't use the bandanna's edges for the edges of the panels; instead, allow extra fabric so that you can hem the edges yourself. (You'll have a neater hem than the bandanna's original one.) To do this, cut the panels from the bandanna, allowing at least ⅝" (1.5 cm) on all edges of the tissue paper pattern (Fig. 27-2).

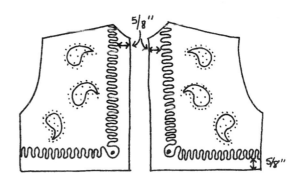

Figure 27-2: When cutting out the front panels, position the bandanna so that the border design is not lost in the seam allowances. Panels should be cut with ⅝" (1.5cm) seam allowances along all edges.

Western Conversion Shirt and Bandanna-Trimmed Shirt

A view of both the original and trimmed shirts illustrates the style and improvements you can add to plain button-front shirts. Fabric yokes edged with removable fringe trim and a fabric-covered collar add western flair to the plain green shirt. Silver button covers complete the transformation. Sections of bandannas decorate a chambray blue shirt. A change to silver buttons with a matching silver concho and silver collar points complete the casual western styling.

4 Fuse the interfacing to the wrong sides of both bandanna panels. Fold under and topstitch the long straight side and bottom edge of each panel (Fig. 27-3). These will be considered the hemmed edges.

Figure 27-3: Wrong side of panel with interfacing applied and straight edges hemmed.

5 Place the panels on the shirt front, pinning them into position in the center and around the hemmed edges (Fig. 27-4).

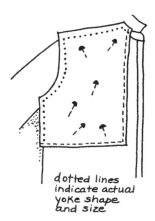

Figure 27-4: Panel pinned to shirt front.

Turn under and pin the raw edges of the panel sides to line up with the shirt at the side seam, sleeve edge, and neck edge. Leave the raw edge exposed at the shoulder, as it will be covered by another bandanna piece. Sew the panel to the shirt, sewing near the folded-under edges of the bandanna. If you don't want the hemmed edges of the panels flipping open on the front of the shirt, sew along those edges too, attaching them to the shirt (Fig. 27-5)

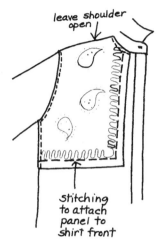

Figure 27-5: The front and bottom edges are stitched to the shirt to hold the panel in place when the shirt is worn.

6 Use the border design on the smaller bandanna for the shoulder covers of the shirt. Measure the length of the shoulder from the neck seam to the top edge of the sleeve (or you can cover the sleeve top past the shoulder seam, as I did). From the bandanna's border design, cut two pieces to this length, plus 1″ (2.5cm) for seam allowances (Fig. 27-6).

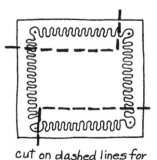

Figure 27-6: Cutting pattern for shoulder cover strips.

Fuse interfacing to the bandanna strips. Pin the center of the shoulder covers to the shirt to position them, then turn under the raw edges on all the edges, pin, and sew to shirt. If the seam allowance on the neck edge of the bandanna strip doesn't cooperate well where you want to turn under the fabric, clip into the seam allowance in a few places.

7 Now cover the shirt cuffs with leftover pieces of the bandannas. The cuffs can match or not: There's no law that says both cuffs must be cut from the same fabric. Though you could interface the bandanna fabric for the cuffs, I chose not to since the denim shirt had fairly bulky cuffs already.

8 Remove the cuff button or buttons. (You may want to change them, as I did.) Cut a piece of bandanna fabric larger than the cuff on all sides. Press under one long edge and pin to the top cuff edge at the sleeve. Turn under and pin the bandanna fabric to meet the cuff sides. Do the same at the cuff bottom edge, or fold the excess fabric around to the inside of the sleeve (Fig. 27-7), which will cover a worn or not-so-fresh-looking cuff edge. If you do this, turn under the bottom raw edge of the cuff cover before sewing it to the cuff. Or zigzag or serge the raw edge from the right side of the cuff cover before pinning the bandanna fabric over the cuff.

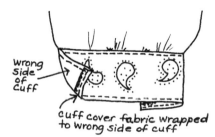

Figure 27-7: Cuff covered with new fabric.

9 To restore the buttonhole, adjust the machine to a very narrow zigzag stitch. Pay attention to the thread color on the bobbin of the machine (since it will show on the cuff), and sew around the original buttonhole from the wrong side of the cuff. Then cut the buttonhole open again. Pretty easy, don't you think? Finally, sew on the button.

Here are some more ideas for western trim: silver collar points, silver buttons (to replace the original ones), and a concho with fringe added to the placket.

Western Conversion Shirt

It's easy to convert a plain shirt to the classy shirt you see on page 86—just right for a night of country line dancing. This shirt would make a great gift for a western wear fan—either male or female. Fringe is added to the shirt front as a removable, changeable feature. Make several different colors and styles of fringe so you can easily change the mood of the shirt. Don't you just love having options! Remove the fringe when laundering the shirt.

SUPPLY LIST

1 PLAIN BUTTON-FRONT SHIRT WITH FRONT POCKETS REMOVED

TISSUE WRAPPING PAPER

½ YD. (46CM) FABRIC FOR SHIRT YOKES AND SHIRT COLLAR COVER

⅛ YD. (11.5CM) FABRIC FOR YOKE TRIM

18″ (46CM) VELCRO, ⅝″ (1/5CM) WIDTH

1 YD. (0.95M) PURCHASED RAYON FRINGE OR FRINGE CUT FROM FABRIC

PAPER-BACKED FUSIBLE WEB

BUTTON COVERS (OPTIONAL)

1 With a washable marker and a straight edge, draw a line on either side of the shirt's front placket, starting at the neck edge and extending down 10″ (25.5cm). Using the same technique, mark a point on each side of the shirt front, just inside where the shoulder seam meets the sleeve seam, and draw a line that extends 4″ (10cm) down from each of these points. Finally, use the straight edge and marker to draw diagonal lines connecting the ends of these two sets of lines, as shown in Figure 27-8. These diagonal lines define the bottom edge of the western yoke. Try the shirt on to determine whether you like the location of this line and the size of the yoke on your body and your shirt. Change the placement of the lines if a smaller or larger yoke would look better.

2 Make a yoke pattern for each side of the shirt, using the pin-tracing method described in Section 6. Cut out the yoke patterns from the fabric, adding extra fabric for seam allowances all around.

Figure 27-8: Size and placement of western yokes on the shirt front.

3 Place the yoke pieces on the shirt body and pin them at the center to hold the fabric to the shirt. Turn under the edges of the yokes and align each folded edge with the appropriate part of the shirt: the sides of the plackets, the diagonal lower lines you drew in Step 1, the sleeve seams, the shoulder seams, or the curved neck edges. If it is difficult to turn under the neck edge of the yoke fabric to match the curve, clip into the seam allowance in two or three places.

4 Next, measure the diagonal line of the yoke bottom edge. This is the length you need for the yoke trim, which also is the attachment area for fringe. Add ½″ (1.3cm) to the measurement and cut two pieces of 2″-wide (5cm) fabric to that length. Fold the pieces in half lengthwise with wrong sides together (Fig. 27-9). Turn under ¼″ (6mm) along the raw edges of each 2″ (5cm) end of the fabric strips and press.

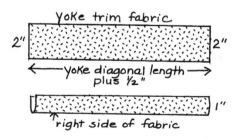

Figure 27-9: Fabric size for yoke trim insert.

5 Measure and cut the Velcro to the same length as one of the yoke trim fabric pieces (minus the folded-under edges). Then cut the strip in half lengthwise. Sew the loop side of the Velcro on the right side of each yoke trim strip near the center fold, as shown in Figure 27-10. I used a medium zigzag stitch.

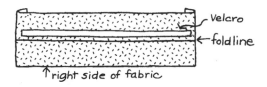

Figure 27-10: Attach the Velcro on trim fabric near the center fold.

6 With the Velcro side of each trim piece facing the shirt, insert the raw edges of the trim beneath the yoke fabric on each side of the shirt so that approximately ½" (1.3cm) of the trim shows (Fig. 27-11). Pin carefully in place and then topstitch along the yoke edges to attach the yoke to the shirt front, attaching the trim to the shirt at the same time.

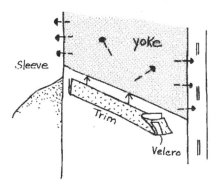

Figure 27-11: Place and pin the trim fabric under the lower edge of the new yoke.

The next step is to add the hook side of the Velcro to the upper edge of the fringe. If you use purchased fringe, add an extra ½" (1.3cm) to the measurement of the trim on the shirt and cut the fringe to that length. Turn ¼" (6mm) of each end to the front of the fringe and sew the hook side of the Velcro to the top edge of the fringe front, using a medium zigzag stitch and catching the turned-under edges in the stitching (Fig. 27-12). The Velcro helps stabilize the fringe top edge. If you are using fabric fringe, turn the ¼" (6mm) on each edge to the *back* of the fringe before attaching the Velcro to the front.

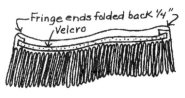

Figure 27-12: The ends of the fringe have been turned back and the Velcro has been sewn to the top edge.

8 I covered the collar of my shirt in a coordinating fabric. A word of warning: Pay attention to the thickness of the original shirt collar and the fabric you plan to add to the top of it. The collar can become very stiff and hard to sew through if you select a thick or crisp fabric as a cover. Trace the shirt collar to make a pattern, and cut the pattern from the fabric, adding seam allowances all around. Turn under the straight edge that meets the collar stand of the shirt and pin this edge to the shirt *collar's* right side (Fig. 27-13).

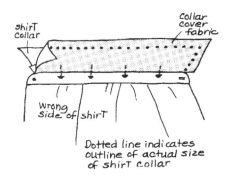

Figure 27-13: The collar cover is pinned in place along edge of the shirt's collar stand.

On this shirt, I decided to wrap the extra fabric to the back of the collar on the sides and top edge. You can zigzag, serge, or apply paper-backed fusible web to the raw edges of the three collar sides. (If you choose to fuse, apply a narrow strip of the paper-backed fusible web, remove the paper, and trim the edge with pinking shears.) Fold the collar fabric around to the wrong side of the collar on all three edges (Fig. 27-14). Pin or press in place. Follow this up with topstitching to hold the fabric cover in place.

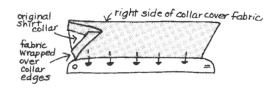

Figure 27-14: The collar fabric is turned under collar's edges and topstiched in place.

You may also want to add fabric to the shirt cuffs, so go ahead (refer to Steps 5–9 in the Tuxedo Shirt with Pillow Panel in Section 25). And maybe you'd also like to cover the shirt's back yoke with a V-shaped fabric piece. Figure 27-15 shows some additional western shapes for a shirt front yoke. I added a set of western-style button covers to the shirt's plain buttons. Don't hesitate to use your own ideas for yoke shapes and western trim.

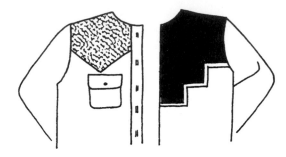

Figure 27-15: Additional yoke shapes for other western conversion shirt projects.

Shirt with Yarn-Couched Ruffle

28

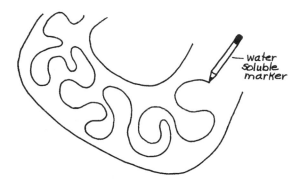

Figure 28-1: Draw a curving line all around the shirt neck ruffle using a washable marking pen.

T rim a ruffled shirt collar with a couching overlay of interesting yarn. Decide if you want the yarn to offer high contrast or tone-on-tone trim, like the shirt shown on page 92. The yarn I used was mohair, but I checked the label to make sure it was washable.

SUPPLY LIST

1 SHIRT OR GARMENT WITH A WIDE RUFFLED COLLAR

YARN FOR COUCHING

TEAR-AWAY STABILIZER OR SPRAY STARCH (OPTIONAL)

1 Draw a pattern to follow with the yarn on the ruffled collar. Use a washable marker, which will allow you to draw lines that are easy to see while you're sewing (Fig. 28-1). Or if you feel artistic and creative, sew without a planned design. Here are some truths to consider as you plan the couching design: straight lines may be easier to sew than tightly curved lines, the design does not have to be perfectly even in all places for this project to be a success, and after couching yarn on one planned design line, you may feel more confident sewing on another line of yarn—freehand and unplanned.

2 Thread color is an option. Though I generally suggest clear nylon thread for an invisible attachment of the yarn, you could use a high contrast color for an added element of trim. Match the bobbin thread to the garment color.

3 Before you begin sewing on the collar, read "What Is Couching" (page 56). Set the sewing machine for a medium-width zigzag stitch and experiment with the yarn, thread color, stitch width, presser foot, and a replica of the design you drew on the ruffle (Fig. 28-2). The time spent in practice will help you decide on the options for this project and give you the confidence to begin sewing on the garment.

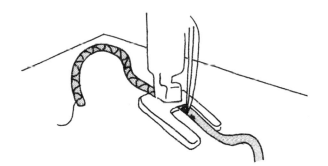

Figure 28-2: Practice sewing the yarn to some test fabric before sewing it onto the collar.

4 Do you need to use a stabilizer under the ruffle? This will depend on the fabric weight. On the featured shirt of medium-weight denim, I did not use a stabilizer but held the shirt fabric taut as I sewed. Naturally, it will be a task to attach a stabilizer all around the ruffle, but on a soft fabric, it will be necessary so that the collar doesn't pucker. Another suggestion for a stabilizer is to use spray starch to stiffen the fabric. Plan to spray the collar several times, allowing the starch to dry between each spraying.

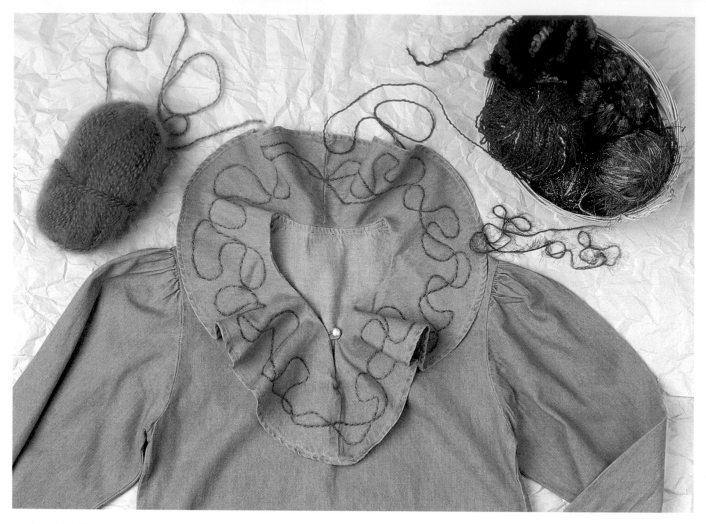

Shirt Ruffle with Yarn Couching
Yarn stitched to the ruffle collar of this shirt is selected from a collection of interesting yarns and sewn or couched into a curving line.

5 To begin stitching on the end of the yarn, sew back and forth to attach the yarn securely. When you return to the starting point to end your couching design, you may want to overlap the yarn over this end (Fig. 28-3). As you are couching the collar, make sure that the yarn source can move freely, whether it is on your lap or in a basket on the floor; avoid sewing a taut line of yarn, which will cause the ruffle to pucker.

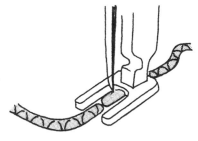

Figure 28-3: Meet or overlap the yarn ends when you've finished stitching your design.

I think you'll discover, as I did, that couching yarn is so much fun that it's hard to stop. After sewing one circle of my planned design, I felt confident enough to add a second line of yarn without drawing another guide. Since perfectly even and regular lines are not required for this project, I felt like an artist sewing yarn in a line wherever I felt like directing my sewing machine needle.

Josephine's Coat of Many Colors

29

Rescue a man's shirt from the rear of the closet, one that is no longer worn by its owner, and turn it into a stunning, colorful, lightweight jacket for yourself. You will use the shirt as a base for sewing on stripes of new fabrics. Some of the stripes on the jacket shown on page 94 have been serged for additional trim. The most important requirement for this project is that the shirt fit you (and is actually a bit large). Think about wearing it over other garments and possibly using shoulder pads. This project was named for both my sister Sarah's former landlady and the female answer to the biblical coat of many colors.

SUPPLY LIST

1 MAN'S BUTTON-FRONT SHIRT

SCRAPS OF FABRIC TO WIDEN SHIRT (IF NEEDED)

1 YD. (0.95M) EACH OF SIX (OR MORE) COORDINATING COTTON FABRICS

ROTARY CUTTER AND MAT (OPTIONAL)

FUSIBLE WEB (OPTIONAL)

EXTRA FABRIC FOR BINDINGS OR FACINGS

1 First let's talk about the shirt you need for this project. Try on the shirt to check the fit around the hip line, the arm length, the armhole size, and the overall length after the shirttails are removed. Is the shirt soft and showing some signs of wear or stains? That won't be a problem, since the entire garment will be covered with other fabric. Is the shirt tapered on the side seams or a straight cut? Check this feature. If you prefer a straight line, you can add

fabric to the shirt front and back to build out the sides (Fig. 29-1). Mark the sleeve length you'll need (plus a little extra) with a pin. You'll be cutting the cuff and excess sleeve length off at the mark.

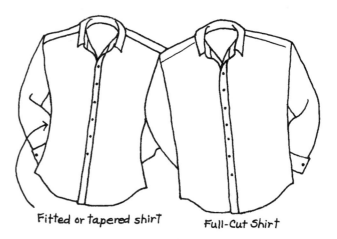

Fitted or tapered shirt   Full-Cut Shirt

Figure 29-1: Two different styles of men's shirts

2 Next, staystitch around the neckline of the shirt right below the collar stand (Fig. 29-2). Then cut off the collar and collar stand, the cuffs and any extra sleeve length, all the buttons on the placket, and the shirttails (Fig. 29-3). You can remove the shirt pockets if you wish, but it's not necessary.

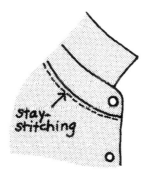

Figure 29-2: Staystitch below the shirt collar stand to preserve the shirt's neckline after you cut off the collar and stand.

Josephine's Coat of Many Colors

Strips of cotton fabrics by P&B, some with serger-stitching trim, are sewn to the base fabric, a man's shirt. The result is an eye-catching lightweight jacket.

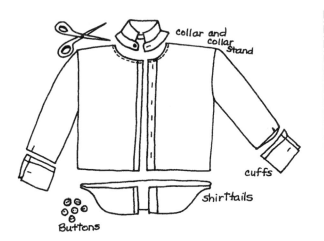

Figure 29-3: Cut off the indicated parts from the shirt and remove the shirt's buttons.

3 Turn the shirt inside out and cut away the seams and seam allowances on the shirt sides and sleeves (Fig. 29-4). Now you can lay the shirt open flat.

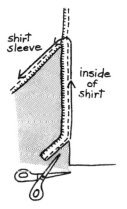

Figure 29-4: The line with the arrows indicates where to cut to remove the seams from the shirt sides and sleeves.

4 At the ends of the shoulder/sleeve seams, you'll notice that the curve in the seam prevents the fabric from lying flat. Make a small tuck, then pin and sew the fabrics in place so they will lie flat at both ends of each sleeve seam (Fig. 29-5).

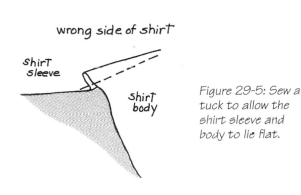

Figure 29-5: Sew a tuck to allow the shirt sleeve and body to lie flat.

Then bring the two sleeve and shirt side edges together and line them up to make sure that the shirt front and back are still the same length now that you have stitched in the tucks. If you plan to extend the shirt sides to form a straight rather than tapered line, sew extra fabric on at this time. Sew the extra fabric so that the seam allowances end up on the *right* of the original shirt fabric (Fig. 29-6).

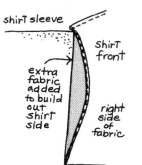

Figure 29-6: Sew extra fabric to the shirt front and back to extend the sides of a tapered shirt.

Also sew the sleeve plackets closed on each sleeve (Fig. 29-7). If there are tucks formed below the shirt's back yoke, sew them closed as well.

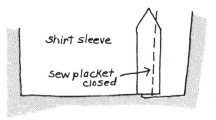

Figure 29-7: Stitch the sleeve plackets closed.

5 Fold the shirt back in half from the neck to the bottom edge, and cut along the fold to cut the back in half. You now have two large pieces to cover with fabric (Fig. 29-8). Set the shirt aside while you cut the strips for covering it.

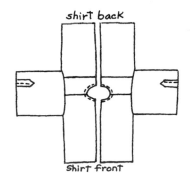

Figure 29-8: The shirt after being cut in half along the center back line.

6 For each of the six colors chosen for this jacket, I cut two 45″ (114cm) long strips of the following widths: 4″ (10cm), 3¼″ (8cm), 2½″ (6.5cm), and 2″ (5cm). Thus for each of the six fabrics, you should have eight strips of varying widths. (Depending on the shirt size and the effect you want to create with the fabric strips, you may need to cut more strips as you proceed with the project.) This cutting is most efficiently done with a rotary cutter on a mat. You may prefer to use a variety of fabrics, many more than six, from your fabric collection. If you do so, cut two of the same width from each fabric.

7 If you'd like to add the detail of serging to some of the strips of fabric, do it before you begin to sew on the strips. With wrong sides of the fabric strips meeting, fold the fabric in half and serge along the fold. This creates a tuck in the fabric strip when it is unfolded (Fig. 29-9). I used a metallic thread in the upper looper to give some "shine" to the stitching.

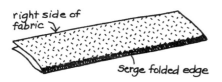

Figure 29-9: Optional serger stitching on the fabric strips.

8 It is very important to lay out the first two fabric pieces on the shirt fronts accurately. With the right side of both shirt fronts facing up, pin on two identical fabric strips extending from the shirt front top center to the back of the shoulder/sleeve seam (Fig. 29-10). Make sure that both pieces are placed on the shirt at the same angle and direction so that the same areas are covered on each side. You will be sewing other fabric strips over both edges of this first one, so if you use numerous pins to secure it to the shirt, you won't have to sew it.

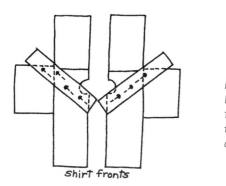

Figure 29-10: Placement of the first fabric strips on the shirt.

9 Match the bobbin thread to the color of the shirt; the top thread should be a neutral shade to blend with the variety of fabric colors you've chosen.

10 Select the next fabric strip to sew onto the shirt front. Align and pin the raw edge of the second strip to the raw edge of the strip pinned to the shirt, with right sides of the fabrics facing. Sew the two strips together and onto the shirt, using a ¼″ (6mm) seam allowance (Fig. 29-11).

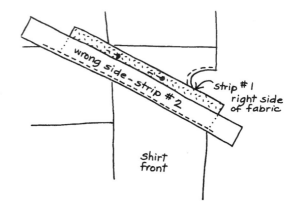

Figure 29-11: With right sides together, align the edges of the fabric strips and sew them together and onto the shirt.

This is the seam allowance you will use for sewing on all the strips. Press the seam allowance flat and then turn the right side of the strip over and press the strip flat (Fig. 29-12). Align the next strip with the second strip in the same manner. Pin and sew the two strips together and onto the shirt.

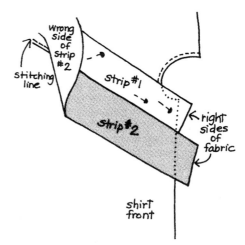

Figure 29-12: After stitching the strip, turn it over so that the right side of the strip fabric is facing up.

11 Proceed in this way to sew and cover one of the shirt fronts and then the other. You will be covering the sleeves at the same time. It is important, for the final design of the jacket, to use strips in the same order of width and color on each side of the shirt front. *Do not cut off the excess fabric on the fabric strips until you have finished covering the shirt with fabric strips.* Due to the angles at which the strips are placed, it's easy to cut the strips too short to cover the shirt edges. I speak from experience.

12 After sewing strips to both shirt fronts, sew strips to the shirt backs, again following the color and fabric width order accurately on each side. To secure the strips to the shirt edges, sew around both halves of the shirt body ⅛" (3mm) from the edge, stitching with the shirt side up. Now trim away the excess fabric from the shirt edges (Fig. 29-13).

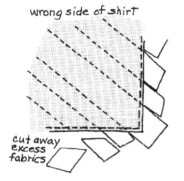

Figure 29-13: After sewing around the edges of both shirt pieces, trim away the extra fabric.

13 Match the two jacket center back edges, with the right sides of the fabric strips facing each other. Pin and sew the shirt back together in one piece. To make the edges of this seam neater inside the jacket, serge or zigzag the edges of the seam allowance or cover the seam with a strip of fabric that has been pinked on the edges and fused in place (Fig. 29-14)

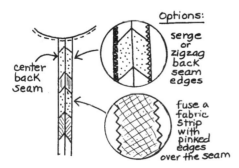

Figure 29-14: Options for treating the center back seam of the jacket.

14 Pin together and sew the jacket sides and sleeve seams, matching right sides of the fabrics. Now try on the jacket to see how it fits before you clean finish the edges. Make any adjustments now.

15 One option for covering the edges of the jacket is to wrap them with binding as I did in the jacket in the photo. The only area needing bias binding is the neckline; the other edges can be wrapped with fabric strips cut on the grain. To finish your jacket like the one in the photo, cut fabric strips 3" (7.5 cm) wide. Fold the strips in half lengthwise with the wrong sides of the fabric together. Align the raw edges of the strips with the raw edges of the jacket fabrics on the shirt side and pin. Sew the binding to the jacket with a ¼" (6mm) seam allowance (Fig. 29-15).

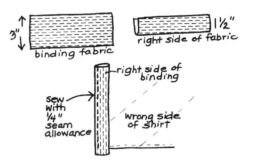

Figure 29-15: Cut a 3"-wide (7.5cm) binding strip, fold in half, and sew to the wrong side of the jacket's edges

Trim the seam allowance and wrap the folded edge of the binding to the right side of the jacket, pin and sew in place near the folded edge of the binding (Fig. 29-16).

right side of jacket

Figure 29-16: The folded edge of binding is turned over to the right side of the jacket, pressed, and sewn in place.

Sew the straight binding strips to the jacket fronts, bottom edges, and sleeves. Then sew a bias binding of the same width to the neck edge, turning under the excess fabric on the ends of the binding before sewing (Fig. 29-17).

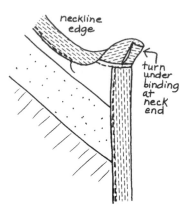

Figure 29-17: Sew binding to the jacket's neck edge.

16 If you prefer facings on your jacket as seen in the photo on the back cover of the book, fold the jacket along the center back and lay the front and neck edges on two pieces of fabric (Fig. 29-18).

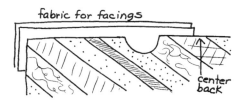

Figure 29-18: Trace the jacket front and neck edge onto the facing fabric.

Trace the outline of the jacket front and neckline, set the jacket aside, and cut the facings 3″ (7.5cm) wide, allowing ¼″ (6mm) seam allowances along the center back edges. Sew the two facings together at the back neck edge. You'll need to cut facings for the ends of the sleeves. Lay the sleeve with wrong sides of the fabric out over a folded piece of fabric (Fig. 29-19). Cut a facing 4″ (10cm) wide if you'd like a cuff edge to fold over. Otherwise, the facing can be cut narrower.

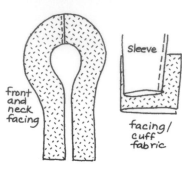

Figure 29-19: Facings for jacket fronts and sleeves.

17 Zigzag, turn under, and stitch, or serge-finish the outer edges of each of the facing pieces (leaving the inside edge of the front-and-neck facing and the upper edge of the cuff facings raw). Then meet the raw edges of the front-and-neck facing to the raw edges of the jacket front and neck edge, with right sides facing. In the same way, align the raw edges of the cuff facings with the cuffs. Pin and sew the facings to the jacket (Fig. 29-20). Trim and clip into the seam allowances, and then turn the facings to the wrong sides of the jacket and press them.

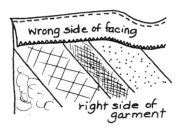

Figure 29-20: Sew the facings to the jacket's edges.

18 Now the only edge left to face is the bottom edge of the jacket. Lay it over a piece of fabric and cut a strip for the bottom edge. This strip could be cut narrower than 3″ (7.5cm) —I suggest trying 1½″ (4cm). Finish the outer edges of this facing and sew it to the jacket as described in Step 17. Turn the facing to the wrong side of the jacket and press it in place. Fuse the top edge of the facing or hand sew, to avoid an obvious stitching line around the jacket. Topstitching ½″ (1.3cm) from the edge of the jacket fronts, neckline, and bottom will hold the facings in place.

The jacket is ready to wear! Have fun in your own Josephine's Coat of Many Colors.

Men's Shirts With Style

30

My advice for decorating garments for males is to be sure to ask them if they like the ideas you're considering for them and if they will wear the garment once it's complete. If there's any hesitation or reluctance, please use your sewing time working on a different idea or for another person.

Man's Shirt with Stepping Rectangles

A simple rectangular shape arranged in steps across a man's shirt was an acceptable applique idea to the man who lives at my house. He also liked the idea of the shapes used on one cuff, and the elbow patches. See the photo on page 100.

SUPPLY LIST

1 MAN'S LONG-SLEEVED, BUTTON-FRONT SHIRT

FABRIC FOR THE APPLIQUE SHAPES

1/4 YD. (23CM) PAPER-BACKED FUSIBLE WEB

1/4 YD. (23CM) STABILIZER

1 This design is an easy one to cut out from paper in order to plan the layout. Cut out a good supply of the rectangles, using the pattern in Figure 30-3 (p. 101), before you begin positioning them on the shirt. Have common pins ready to hold the paper shapes in place.

2 If the shirt has a pocket on the right side, as most men's shirts do, begin the design layout on the left side of the top edge of the pocket, as shown in Figure 30-1. One of the next rectangles will be placed across the shirt placket; this piece should cross between buttonholes. On the left side of the shirt, some of the rectangles are sewn over the bottom edge of the pocket. If this is not acceptable to you or to the person who will wear the shirt, plan the design to avoid overlapping the pocket.

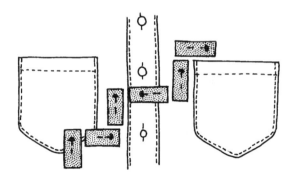

Figure 30-1: Suggested rectangle arrangement for the shirt front.

3 Extend the design to the cuff, if you wish (Fig. 30-2). Another area you could decorate is the shirt's back yoke. Use the paper rectangles to help you determine how many appliques you want to add to the shirt.

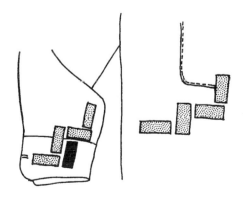

Figure 30-2: Rectangles added to the cuff.

Men's Shirts with Style

Geometric shapes were selected for the trim on both of the men's shirts featured in this photo. Cotton fabric selected for the blue shirt creates an off-set frame for the pocket and triangles that are sewn to the shirt placket. The same triangle shapes are sewn on the back of the shirt, across the bottom of the shirt yoke. On the purple shirt, appliqued rectangles of imitation suede fabric step diagonally across the shirt front and extend to the sleeve and cuff areas. Elbow patches of matching fabric are also sewn to the shirt—a special request of the man who will wear the shirt.

4 After you have pinned the paper rectangles to the shirt, show it to the person who will wear it. Also show him the fabrics and colors you intend to use for the appliques. Listen carefully to the response and proceed accordingly.

5 Trace the rectangle shapes onto paper-backed fusible web and fuse them to the wrong side of the applique fabric. Cut out the rectangles and remove the paper backing from them to begin planning your layout. If you're using imitation suede cloth, Ultrasuede, or another fabric with a nap, pay special attention to the nap direction as you plan the layout of the rectangles. By placing the cut rectangles in opposite directions, the applique fabric will seem to have different shadings. When you've decided on the effect you want to create and have finalized the layout, fuse the rectangles to the shirt.

6 Some men's shirts are made of very firm, light canvas-type fabrics; if yours is, you may be able to skip using a stabilizer. Make sure you test sew before deciding. Otherwise, pin stabilizer to the wrong side of the shirt behind all of the stitching areas before starting to sew.

7 The appliques on the shirt in the photo were attached with black thread, using a decorative machine stitch along the edges. This is a noticeable part of the design, which you may prefer to change. A suggestion for the stitch to use around the rectangles is shown in Figure 30-4, but don't let it limit your choices.

V-^-v-^-v-^-v-^-v-^-v-^-v

Figure 30-4: One stitch choice for sewing the rectangle appliques to the shirt.

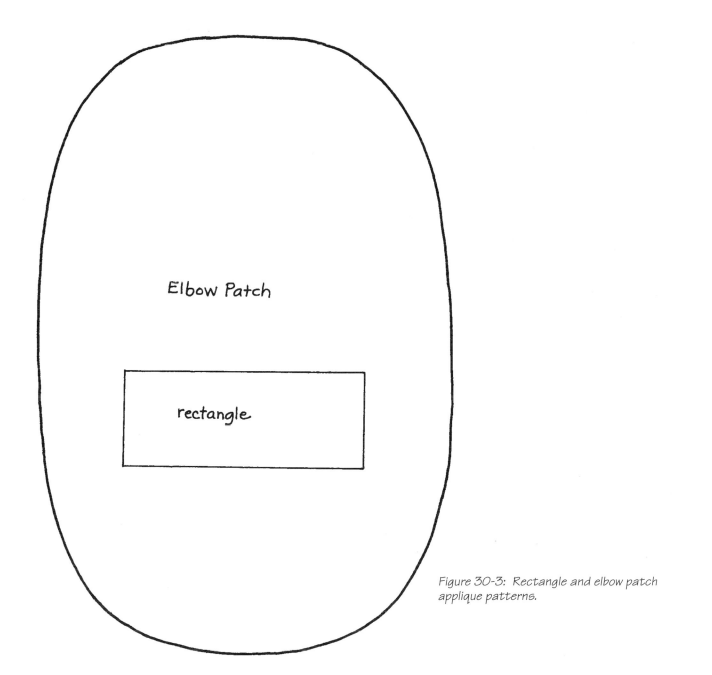

Elbow Patch

rectangle

Figure 30-3: Rectangle and elbow patch applique patterns.

8 Now, about those elbow patches. The pattern for the elbow patches is included in Figure 30-3. It was designed so two patches could be cut from a 9 x 6″ (23 x 15cm) piece of fabric. The patches are really just appliques. Trace the shape onto paper-backed fusible web two times and fuse the web pieces to the wrong side of the elbow patch fabric. Cut the two patches from the fabric. Getting the patches in the right position on the shirt sleeve is important (Fig. 30-5). Elbow patches that are in the middle of the upper arm look a bit ridiculous. If possible, have the man who will wear the shirt try it on and mark the point of his elbow. This center mark will help you to position the elbow patch on the sleeve.

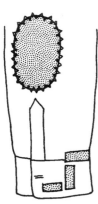

Figure 30-5: Place the elbow patches accurately on the sleeves.

9 Peel off the paper backing and fuse the patches to the shirt sleeves. Next, add stabilizer inside the sleeve behind the patch area, and prepare to sew. Maneuvering the sleeve so that you can sew in the elbow area is truly a fabric manipulation project. The larger the man's shirt, the more room you'll have to work in. The fastest way to sew the patches is to use a straight stitch. This works well if the fabric is nonfraying, such as suede cloth or Ultrasuede. Otherwise, use the same decorative stitch you used to sew on the rectangles.

If you have followed men's fashions in recent years, you've realized that men's wear is now available in a wide range of colors. Of course, you need to consider the man for whom you are decorating a shirt and his acceptance level for colors and designs. This knowledge will help as you plan any shirt-decorating project.

Man's Shirt with Pocket Frame and Triangles

Geometrics are a safe applique category for most men, so the blue shirt on page 100 features triangles on both the front placket and also across the shirt's back yoke (see Figure 30-10). One of the pockets is also framed by another piece of fabric. This trim idea can solve the problem of a good shirt that has ink marks above the pocket opening.

SUPPLY LIST

1 MAN'S BUTTON-FRONT SHIRT

$1/4$ YD. (23CM) FABRIC FOR APPLIQUES AND POCKET TRIM

$1/4$ YD. (23CM) PAPER-BACKED FUSIBLE WEB

$1/4$ YD. (23CM) STABILIZER

1 As you plan this shirt conversion, show your ideas and plans to the man who will wear the shirt. Paper cutouts of the design shapes will help you explain your ideas before you actually cut the shapes from fabric (refer to Steps 1 and 4 in Man's Shirt with Stepping Rectangles, earlier in this section).

2 With a seam ripper, remove the pocket from the shirt. Cut a square of fabric larger than the pocket for the pocket frame (Fig. 30-6).

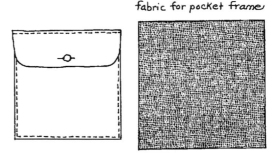

Figure 30-6: The shirt pocket and a larger piece of fabric that will form the frame.

Turn under the edges, press, and position the extra fabric on the shirt. The shirt in the photo has the frame placed at an angle. Sew the frame to the shirt and then position and sew the pocket over the top of the frame (Fig. 30-7).

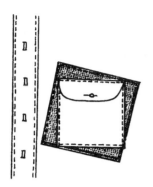

Figure 30-7:
The pocket has been reattached to shirt with the frame beneath it.

3 Trace the triangle pattern in Figure 30-8 onto paper and cut it out. Trace the paper pattern onto paper-backed fusible web. Make as many triangles as you will need for your design. Fuse the shapes to the wrong side of the fabric and cut them out of the fabric. Remove the paper backing from the fabric triangles, position them on the shirt, and fuse them in place.

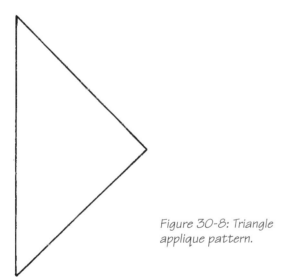

Figure 30-8: Triangle applique pattern.

On my shirt, the triangle closest to the shirt neckline was trimmed before it was fused so that it fit better in the space on the placket (Fig. 30-9).

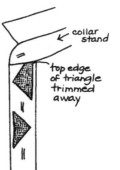

Figure 30-9: Before fusing, trim the top of the upper triangle to fit in the space between the buttonhole and the shirt collar stand.

4 Place one strip of stabilizer behind the shirt placket and one behind the back yoke. Sew the shapes to the shirt, stitching along the edges of the triangles. The choices of stitch and thread color are yours to make. I used a traditional satin stitch for this project and matched the thread to the fabric (Fig. 30-10).

Figure 30-10: Triangles sewn across the shirt's back yoke.

It's always best to consult with a man before trimming a shirt for him. If his response to your ideas is lukewarm, either propose another idea or decide to trim garments for someone else.

Jackets
Part Six

Jacket Lapels with Battenberg Lace

31

Figure 31-1: Battenberg lace pieces cut apart and ready to attach to jacket lapels.

A plain suit jacket can be rejuvenated with a supply of Battenberg lace motifs and just a little bit of sewing (see the jacket on p. 106). This feminine touch gives an extraordinary look to an otherwise ordinary jacket. The coordinating lapel pin is a combination of more lace pieces, buttons, and ribbon loops.

SUPPLY LIST

1 JACKET WITH LAPELS

BATTENBERG LACE INSERTS OR YARDAGE TO TRIM LAPEL AND COLLAR

¹⁄₄ YD. (23CM) LIGHTWEIGHT FUSIBLE INTERFACING (OPTIONAL)

2 BATTENBERG DOILIES, 3" (7.5CM) IN DIAMETER

ASSORTED BUTTONS AND RIBBON OR CORDING FOR THE LAPEL PIN

1 Collect a variety of Battenberg lace pieces and spend some time planning the placement of the lace around the jacket lapels. On the jacket in the photo, two large lace pieces were cut in half to make four pieces of lapel trim for the front of the jacket and one smaller lace doily was also cut in half and used at the center back of the collar (Fig. 31-1).

2 After planning the arrangement of the lace pieces, carefully cut apart the lace motifs and pin the cut edges to the wrong side of the jacket lapels. For extra protection for the cut edges, fuse narrow strips of lightweight fusible interfacing over them before sewing the trim in place on the lapels (Fig. 31-2).

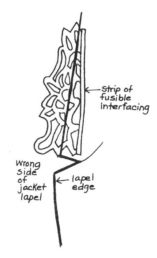

Figure 31-2: A strip of fusible interfacing protects the cut edge of the Battenberg lace.

3 Select a thread color that closely matches the topstitching thread on the jacket lapel and then sew along the topstitching seam already on the lapels or add another row of stitching.

4 For the extra lapel trim shown on the jacket, use the two small Battenberg doilies. The white doily I used is heart shaped. Stitch the first doily to the jacket lapel with a basting stitch around the center of the doily (Fig. 31-3).

Figure 31-3: Attach the first small doily to the jacket's lapel.

5 I dyed the center doily pink to match my jacket. Gather the second doily at the center to give another dimension to the lapel trim. Sew with a gathering stitch around the center (Fig. 31-4).

Figure 31-4: Sew around the second small doily with a gathering stitch. Pull the stitches together to create a flowerlike shape.

In some parts of the center there may be no lace to sew on, but continue to sew in a circle and you'll find that the stitching will gather together when you pull the threads. Knot the threads to retain the gathering. Collect some interesting shank-style buttons and sew them by hand to the center of the right side of the gathered doily. Also sew, by hand or by machine, some loops of coordinating yarn, ribbon, and/or cord to the center of the doily. Using a safety pin, pin the decorated gathered doily to the center of the first doily from the wrong side of jacket lapel.

If you like the idea of trimming the edge of jacket lapels, consider using the zigzag design idea in the Southwest-Style Denim Jacket in Section 33.

Jacket Lapels with Battenberg Lace
Battenberg lace insets (from Wimpole Street Creations) are cut apart and sewn to this jacket to add a feminine touch to the straight edges of the lapels. Smaller doilies (one of them dyed pink with Dritz Dylon dye), a button collection, and ribbons create fabric jewelry on the lapel.

Suit Jacket with Appliques

32

The gray wool suit jacket shown on page 108 was a plain but classic find at a consignment store. It reminded me of some of the outfits and suits we all have in our closets: garments too good to give away but not being worn. If you've saved these clothes because of the high quality of the fabric and/or garment, it's worth considering a renovation or decoration to give them new life. On my suit jacket, three applique shapes in Ultrasuede coordinate with the black cording on the edges of the jacket.

SUPPLY LIST

1 PLAIN SUIT JACKET, CARDIGAN-STYLE

¼ YD. (23CM) PAPER-BACKED FUSIBLE WEB

ONE 9″ (23CM) SQUARE OF BLACK ULTRASUEDE FOR THE APPLIQUES

¼ YD. (23CM) TEAR-AWAY STABILIZER

SCRAP FABRIC FOR APPLIQUE CENTERS (OPTIONAL)

1 Trace the applique design from Figure 32-2 (p. 109) onto paper three times and cut out. When I was experimenting with designs for this jacket, I cut the applique shapes from black construction paper to get a more realistic view of the design.

2 Positioning the paper designs on the jacket front is a little like playing. Even after I chose the applique design for the jacket, I did not know where I would place the shapes. It was one of those "Aha!" moments when I realized that the hole in the design could encircle the button and buttonhole (Fig. 32-1). I felt

inspired! If the buttonholes and buttons on your suit are larger than mine, you can enlarge the hole within the design. One of my first ideas for trimming the jacket was to place one of the applique shapes over the shoulder and extend it to the jacket front. This placement would have worked, but the shoulder pad was in the way. If you really want to use an over-the-shoulder design on a jacket with shoulder pads, you can open the jacket's inside lining at the hem edge, temporarily remove the shoulder pad(s), stitch on the appliques, and then replace everything. If that sounds like too much work, consider hand sewing the appliques in place.

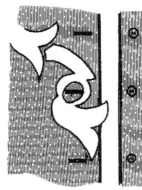

Figure 32-1: Applique design with hole surrounding the buttonhole.

3 After deciding on the number and placement of the applique designs, mark the placement on the jacket with pins. Next, trace the shapes onto paper-backed fusible web and fuse the shapes to the wrong side of the Ultrasuede. Cut out the shapes from Ultrasuede, remove the paper backing from each shape, and carefully fuse the appliques to the garment. Use a press cloth over the Ultrasuede to preserve the sueded surface. When setting the iron temperature for fusing, don't forget to consider the fabric of the suit jacket. It would be a good idea to use a press cloth on most suit jacket fabrics. For the holes in the two appliques without a button in the center, I fused a small circle of extra fabric directly onto the jacket and then fused the applique shape on top of the circle (Fig. 32-3).

Suit Jacket with Appliques

Black Ultrasuede appliques complement the classic, sophisticated style of a wool jacket. The Ultrasuede purse is by Ghee's.

Figure 32-2: Applique pattern.

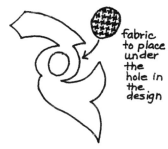

fabric to place under the hole in the design

Figure 32-3: A fabric circle is fused beneath the hole of the applique.

4 Before sewing on the appliques, make sure to add tear-away stabilizer to the wrong side of the jacket. A tear-away variety is important for this project, considering again the nature of the suit fabric. (Water-soluble and rinse-away varieties would not be wise choices for non-washable jackets.) Even though the suit jacket is of firm fabric and has a lining, a stabilizer is still needed to prevent the stitching from puckering the base fabric.

5 Choose a stitch for the applique and stitch around all of the edges of each applique, including the circle in the middle. On my jacket, I used a straight stitch and black thread, since I did not want the stitching to be a noticeable part of the design. The color of the thread and the stitch you select can add extra detail around the design, which you might want for your jacket.

Now that you've seen my jacket and read the instructions, I hope you will find your own plain cardigan-style suit jacket to trim.

Southwest-Style Denim Jacket

33

Trim a casual denim jacket with new yokes and Ultrasuede accents. Not only does this trim give the jacket a different look, it also covers some of the areas that are hard to keep clean.

SUPPLY LIST

1 DENIM JEANS-STYLE JACKET

1/2 YD. (46CM) FABRIC FOR YOKE TRIM

1/4 YD. (23CM) ULTRASUEDE OR LARGE SCRAP PIECES OF ULTRASUEDE FOR THE POCKETS, COLLAR, BACK YOKE, AND CUFFS

1/4 YD. (23CM) PAPER-BACKED FUSIBLE WEB

1 The first step of this jacket transformation is to make patterns for each of the areas you will cover with new fabric. Use the pin-tracing technique in Section 6 to make patterns for both front yokes, the back yoke, the front pocket flaps, and the collar (Fig. 33-1).

make patterns for all jacket areas shown in gray.

Figure 33-1: The gray areas will be covered with new fabrics

(My sister Sarah asked me to cover the collar since that's an especially difficult area to keep clean on the white jacket she wears. It pays to listen to someone with practical experience.)

2 Select fabric for the yokes. I chose a medium-weight tapestry-style fabric and found that it worked well, but a thicker fabric would have been a problem. Since you will be sewing the extra fabric to layers of denim, which is already thick, select fabric that is not too stiff, crisp, or thick. Cut the yoke patterns from the fabric, leaving a generous 5/8" (1.5cm) seam allowance beyond the borders of the pattern pieces (Fig. 33-2). My experience is that it's much easier to trim away excess fabric than to try to turn under a tiny seam allowance, or worse yet, have to cut a whole new piece for the yoke.

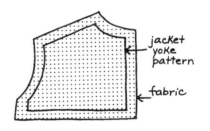

jacket yoke pattern

fabric

Figure 33-2: When cutting out the patterns from the material, add seam allowances.

3 Cut the fabric covers for the pocket flaps next. I used Ultrasuede and pinked the rounded edges of the flap. The Ultrasuede is cut only slightly larger than the pattern, since the edges are not turned under. Extra fabric is allowed at the top straight edge of the flaps, which will be sewn under the yoke cover fabric (Fig. 33-3).

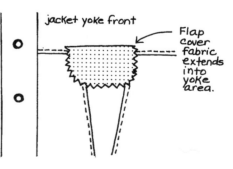

jacket yoke front

Flap cover fabric extends into yoke area.

Figure 33-3: Pocket flap cover.

Denim Jacket with Weaving, Fringe, and Reflectors and Southwest-Style Denim Jacket
Denim strips from old jeans are serged and woven together for the unique shoulder trim on the blue denim jacket from Alpha Shirt Company (Section 34). Small squares of Scotchlite reflective material stitched to the weaving, collar, and cuffs make this jacket and its wearer visible in the dark. Southwest printed fabric and solid-color Ultrasuede turn a white denim jacket into a garment with style (Section 33).

4 Pin or fuse the fabric to the top of the pocket flap to hold the fabric in place. Make sure the top edge of the flap cover fabric extends into the yoke area above. Sew around the curved edges. If you do not plan to use the jacket pockets, you could sew the flaps flat to the jacket front. Otherwise, note that it will be a bit awkward to sew the top of the flap, due to the thicknesses of fabric. Cut a buttonhole in the flap by cutting from the underside through the existing hole. Because the Ultrasuede is a non-fraying fabric, it won't be necessary to sew around the buttonhole.

5 Ultrasuede trim can be added to the bottom of the back yoke edge, as shown in Figure 33-4. Copy the V-pattern for the trim (p. 113) onto paper and then cut the piece from the Ultrasuede. Sew the top straight edge of the trim to the back yoke edge before covering the back yoke with fabric.

Figure 33-4: V-shaped trim sewn to edge of jacket's back yoke

6 Although you can cover either the back or the front yokes first, we'll start with the front yokes. First work with the yoke on the side with the jacket's buttons. Pin the yoke cover fabric to the jacket in the center area. Turn under and pin the sleeve side and bottom edge. Clip into the seam allowances if the fabric is reluctant to turn under in a curved line. Since the buttons on most denim jackets are permanent and cannot be removed to attach a new jacket yoke, it is important to plan for this before sewing on the new yoke. When you know where the yoke will cover the buttons on the jacket, fuse 1" (2.5cm) square pieces of paper-backed fusible web to the wrong side of the yoke cover directly over the button areas (Fig. 33-5). Peel off the paper and cut a line in the fused area just large enough to get the button through. Fuse the edges of the fabric in place around the buttons to avoid raveling.

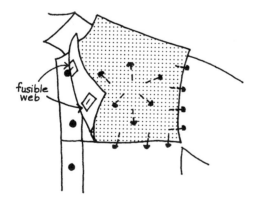

Figure 33-5: Apply paper-backed fusible web to the yoke fabric on the area directly over the buttons. Remove the paper, cut the opening, and slip the buttons through. Then immediately fuse the cut edges to the jacket.

7 Continue turning under and pinning along the edges of the yoke fabric. At the shoulder edge, leave the excess fabric overlapping the shoulder line. Topstitch around the edges of the yoke fabric cover.

8 The yoke cover for the side with the buttonholes is pinned and sewn to the jacket in the same manner as the other front yoke. You don't have to accommodate the buttonholes until after the yoke is sewn in place. After the yoke cover has been sewn in place, make the new buttonholes. On the wrong side of the jacket front, stitch with a narrow zigzag stitch around the existing buttonholes. Cut the holes into the new fabric from behind (Fig. 33-6).

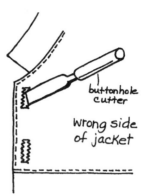

Figure 33-6: Cut the buttonholes through the new fabric after stitching around them with a narrow zigzag stitch.

9 Next we'll cover the jacket's back yoke. Pin the fabric cover to the jacket in the yoke's center. Turn under and pin the bottom, sides, and neckline edges of the fabric. At the shoulder seams, turn under the fabric and cover the raw edges of the front yoke pieces. Topstitch the yoke cover in place (Fig. 33-7).

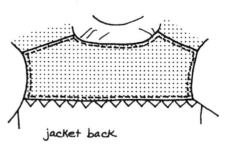

Figure 33-7: The jacket's back yoke has been covered, and the new fabric has been stitched in place.

10 Cut the collar pattern from the Ultrasuede; cut the fabric slightly larger than the pattern. My jacket collar has pinked edges. I used a straight stitch to attach the collar cover to the original collar. Pin or fuse the fabric to the jacket collar and then sew to attach permanently.

11 Cover the edges of the cuffs for a nice touch and also to help keep the jacket looking cleaner longer (Fig. 33-8).

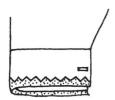

Figure 33-8: Sew fabric to the cuff's edges to coordinate with the other jacket trim and to help keep the jacket clean.

Cut two strips of Ultrasuede 1½" (3cm) wide and as long as the cuff edge. You may wish to pink one edge of the strip, as I did. With the right side of the fabric to the wrong side of the cuff edge, sew the fabric to the cuff with a ¼" seam allowance (Fig. 33-9). Turn the fabric to the right side of the cuff and sew near the top edge to attach the cuff cover to the jacket.

Figure 33-9: First sew the cuff cover to the wrong side of the jacket's cuff, and then turn it over to the right side and sew it in place.

The changes you've added to your denim jacket are sure to attract attention. They turn an ordinary garment into something extraordinary.

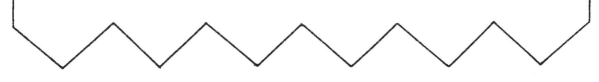

Extend this "v" pattern for trim along the jacket back yoke.

V-pattern for the jacket's back yoke.

Denim Jacket with Weaving, Fringe, and Reflectors

34

Treat the shoulder of a denim jacket with this unusual display of woven denim strips and fringe and patches of Scotchlite reflective material (Fig. 34-1). Like the idea, but you don't wear denim jackets? I suggest other uses for this trim at the end of the project's directions.

Figure 34-1: Serged strips of denim from old blue jeans are woven together and enhanced with squares of Scotchlite reflective material for an unusual shoulder trim on this denim jacket. Additional reflective squares are stitched to the collars and cuffs.

1. Measure the width of the shoulder area on the jacket you'll be trimming. To that measurement, add 2" (5cm). For the jacket in the photo, I cut five denim strips to go across the shoulder area. Each of the pieces were cut 1¼" (3cm) wide and, after serging, they measured 1" (2.5cm) wide (Fig. 34-2).

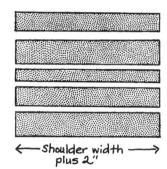

← shoulder width →
plus 2"

Figure 34-2: Measure the jacket's shoulder width and add 2" (5cm). Cut the shoulder strips to this length.

2. Before cutting the strips of fringe that will be woven through the shoulder pieces, determine how long you want the strips to extend beyond the weaving. Do you want the strips to all be the same length? Do you want the strips to hang down the back of the jacket? On my jacket, five strips of various widths are woven through and allowed to hang as fringe on both the front and back of the jacket. The strips were all cut from different pairs of old blue jeans and I turned over some of them to show the reverse side of the denim, which resulted in several different shades of blue. After you have decided on the length of the fringe strips, add 2 to 3" (5 to 7.5cm) if you want to tie knots in the ends of them (see Step 8). Cut the denim strips.

3 I serged the edges of all the denim strips. You could sew along the edges with a zigzag stitch or just let the denim unravel along the edges. Serge the short ends before you serge the long edges of the strips (Fig. 34-3). I used a three-thread rolled edge stitch. If you serge the ends, apply Fray Check to the corners, and allow the strips to dry. Then trim off the thread tails. Press all the strips before weaving them.

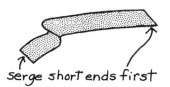

serge short ends first

Figure 34-3: Serge the short ends of the strips first, then the long edges.

4 Pin the right ends of the shorter, shoulder strips to your ironing board. Begin the weaving at least ½" (1.3cm) away from the right edge (Fig. 34-4).

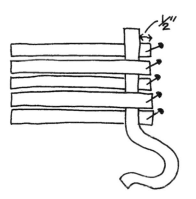

Figure 34-4: Pin the shoulder strips to the ironing board and begin weaving the longer strips through them, leaving ½" (1.3cm) free along the right edge.

Weave the longer strips through the shoulder strips. You can leave gaps in the weaving if you want the jacket fabric to be seen beneath. To secure the weaving, pin the outer layered areas together at the points shown in Figure 34-5. Lay the woven piece over the jacket shoulder to test the size and fit of your creation so far. This is most easily done if the jacket is on a dressmaker's model or on another person.

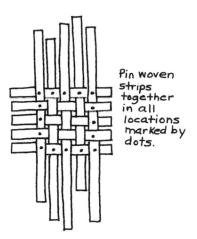

Pin woven strips together in all locations marked by dots.

Figure 34-5: To hold the weaving together, pin layered areas at the points indicated.

5 When the piece is adjusted to the right size, turn under the extra fabric on the shoulder width pieces and sew the folded edges in place with clear nylon thread (Fig. 34-6). Trim away the excess denim on the back side of the weaving, trimming close to the stitching line.

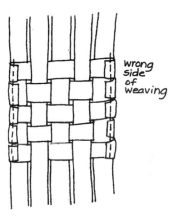

wrong side of weaving

Figure 34-6: The wrong side of the weaving after the edges of the shoulder strips have been turned under and stitched in place and the seam allowances have been trimmed.

6 It's a good idea to add the squares of Scotchlite reflective material to the weaving at this time, before you fuse the unit to the jacket. First, add paper-backed fusible web to the Scotchlite and cut out squares that will fit onto the squares defined by the weaving. Then, remove the paper backing from the squares and fuse them to the weaving. I chose to cover random squares on the weaving and to add a few squares on the collar and cuffs of the jacket, as shown in the photos of the jacket. Use clear nylon thread and a narrow zigzag stitch to secure the Scotchlite patches (Fig. 34-7). Now, when the jacket is worn at night, or on a darkened dance floor, the squares will reflect light.

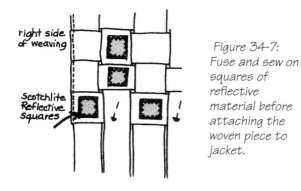

Figure 34-7: Fuse and sew on squares of reflective material before attaching the woven piece to jacket.

7 Now position the decorated woven unit on the shoulder of the jacket and pin it carefully in place. Attach it to the jacket by topstitching along the outside edges of the weaving, using a jeans needle in the sewing machine. At some places you will be sewing through many layers of denim, so it's best to sew slowly.

8 If you find the ends of the fringe curl up more than you'd like, knot the ends or turn under the bottom edges and sew or fuse them down to give them more weight (Fig. 34-8).

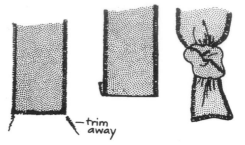

Figure 34-8: Here are some options for finishing the ends of the woven fringe.

The decorative woven accent can be applied to both shoulders of the jacket. Different colors of fabric for the strips would add another detail of interest. You could also use a nonfraying fabric such as Ultrasuede for the weaving and eliminate the serging or sewing on the edges of the strips.

Try this technique on other kinds of jackets too. An unlined blazer or casual jacket (see the photo on the book's back cover) looks terrific with a woven shoulder cover, which could be used to hide a worn or stained area. Remove the shoulder pad before doing the sewing and reattach it later. Instead of serging the edges of the strips, turn under and sew (or fuse the four edges of each strip for a nearly-no-sew option). You could even fuse the whole woven piece to the jacket without doing any stitching at all.

*Sweaters
& Dresses
Part Seven*

Patchwork Sweater 35

Patches of suede cloth and Ultrasuede were used to create this geometric design on a man's sweater. One of the patches covers an embroidered logo on the garment. Of course, this idea would work on a woman's sweater too.

SUPPLY LIST

1 PULLOVER SWEATER

¼ YD. (23CM) PAPER-BACKED FUSIBLE WEB

AN ASSORTMENT OF FABRICS FOR THE PATCHES

¼ YD. (23CM) STABILIZER

1 If your sweater has a logo you'd like to cover with a patch, measure the logo to determine how large the covering patch needs to be. To cover the logo on my sweater, I cut rectangles 2½" x 3½" (6.5 x 9cm) (Fig. 35-1).

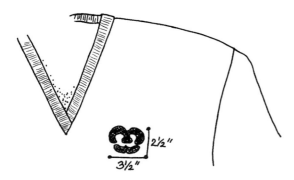

Figure 35-1: Measure the logo or area you want to cover with patchwork.

2 Trace rectangles onto paper-backed fusible web, fuse them to the wrong sides of the chosen fabrics, cut them out, and remove the paper backing.

3 Naturally, you'll start arranging the patchwork design by covering the logo first. Use the design on the sweater in the photo, or build your own overlapping pattern. Pin the rectangles in place and try on the sweater to get a good look at the design. When you've finalized the layout, fuse the shapes to the sweater, being careful not to stretch the sweater as you work.

4 Here's a way to prepare the rectangles for this project that doesn't require paper-backed fusible web. Use your serger to stitch around all four sides of the fabric rectangles. (You should cut them slightly larger to prepare for serging.) Use fusible thread in the lower looper of the serger to make the rectangles easy to secure to the sweater (Fig. 35-2). Trim and secure the thread tails on the ends of the rectangles. When you have the shapes arranged on the sweater, fuse them in place.

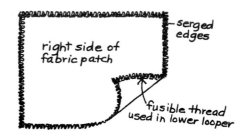

Figure 35-2: Serge the edges of your patches using fusible thread on the wrong side of the fabric. This will make it easy and quick to fuse the patch to the sweater.

5 On a sweater, it's especially important to add stabilizer to the wrong side of the garment before sewing. Pin or otherwise attach the stabilizer to the wrong side of the sweater in the area where the appliques will be attached. Select a machine stitch to sew around the shapes (Fig. 35-3). I used a stitch that reminded me of serger stitching, which led me to think of the technique described in Step 4. If you've used the serger method described in Step 4, choose thread that matches the serger thread and sew in the area of the serger stitches. After the stitching is complete, remove the stabilizer, and press the sweater from the wrong side.

Figure 35-3: I used this sewing machine stitch for sewing the patches to my sweater.

If it's not a logo to cover, perhaps it's a stain or ink mark. You'll find this patchwork trim quick and easy to add. If you like the look of this sweater, you might want to try the Patchwork Shirt with Placket Cover in Section 26.

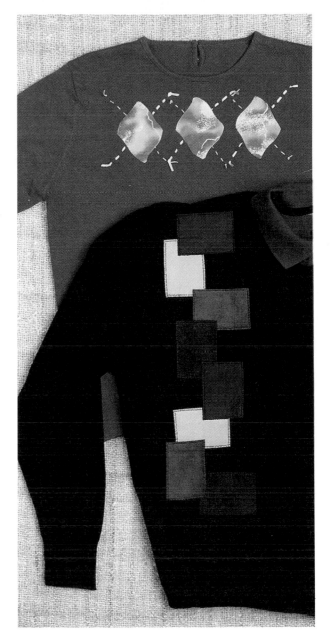

Sweater with Weaving & Lined Argyle Applique and Patchwork Sweater

On the short-sleeve sweater, a curvy edge argyle applique pattern is enhanced with narrow ribbons woven through the sweater knit (Section 36). Overlapping patches of suede cloth embellish one side of a plain long-sleeve sweater that can be worn by a man or a woman (section 35).

Sweater with Lined Argyle Applique

36

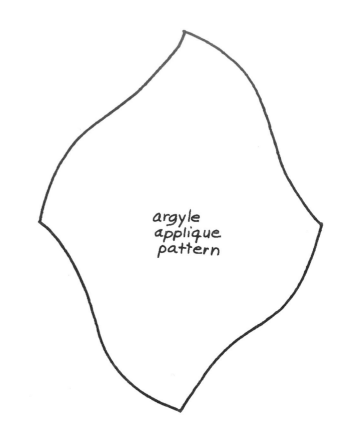

Figure 36-2: Argyle applique pattern.

T wo sewing techniques are combined on this sweater: appliques lined with lightweight fusible interfacing and ribbons woven through the sweater knit to create an argyle pattern (Fig. 36-1).

SUPPLY LIST

1 PULLOVER SWEATER

PAPER FOR TEMPLATES

ONE 9 X 6″ (23 X 15CM) PIECE OF LIGHTWEIGHT FUSIBLE INTERFACING (TRICOT KNIT)

ONE 9 X 6″ (23 X 15CM) PIECE OF FABRIC FOR THREE APPLIQUES

1/4 YD. (23CM) STABILIZER

1 YD. (0.95M) NARROW RIBBON FOR WEAVING

1 Try a new method of lined applique for this sweater project. Trace the off-set argyle diamond shape from Figure 36-2, and cut out the pattern from paper. Trace the pattern three times onto the wrong side of the applique fabric, leaving a space between each pattern. Place the right side of the applique fabric to the fusible side of the interfacing, pin the fabrics together, and sew around the three argyle shapes, using the lines you drew as the stitching lines (Fig. 36-3).

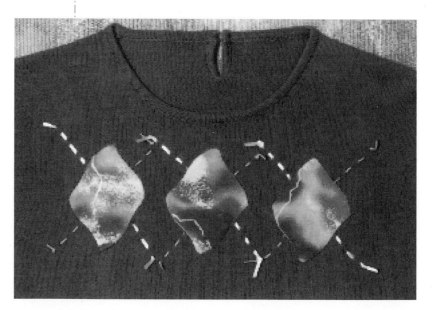

Figure 36-1: Add interesting textures and dimension to a flat knit sweater with lined fabric appliques and woven ribbons used to create an argyle design.

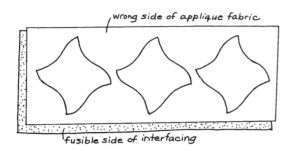

Figure 36-3: Sew the applique fabric to fusible interfacing to create lined appliques.

2 Cut around each shape, leaving ⅛" seam allowance. Also clip into the seam allowance. To save time and accomplish both steps at once, use pinking shears to cut out the shapes. Cut a 1" (2.5cm) slash in the interfacing and pull the right sides of the fabric out through the hole (Fig. 36-4). Finger press the edges of the fabric or press the shapes on an applique pressing sheet or leftover paper backing from which the fusible web has been removed. The interfacing side will not stick permanently to the Teflon applique pressing sheet or the paper.

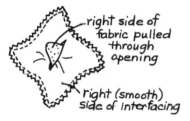

Figure 36-4: Turn the applique right side out through a cut in the interfacing.

3 Before fusing the shapes to the sweater, determine the locations of the appliques by trying on the sweater and pinning the shapes to the sweater front. Once you've decided on the layout of the shapes, take off the sweater and fuse the designs in place, being careful not to stretch the sweater. The fusing material on the applique lining allows you to attach the shapes without using paper-backed fusible web. You might appreciate the soft, not stiff, feel of these appliques and use this method on other garments as well.

4 Add stabilizer to the wrong side of the sweater beneath the design area. Select a stitch such as the blanket or blind hem stitch and adjust the machine to sew a narrow width. Use clear nylon thread as the top thread and match the bobbin thread to the garment color. Sew along the edges of the design shapes, so that the stitching catches the shapes only when the needle swings to the left. With clear thread this will be a hidden, hard-to-see stitching line. After the sewing is complete, remove the stabilizer and press the sweater from the wrong side to flatten the appliques.

5 The lines of the traditional argyle pattern are created with narrow ribbon woven through the sweater knit. The needle you use for hand weaving should have a large eye and a blunt end or have an eye at each end. Place a knot near the end of the ribbon and lace it through the sweater toward the argyle patch. Make sure to leave some give in the ribbon, that is, don't pull it too tightly. Continue the weaving on the opposite side of the argyle, as shown in Figure 36-5. The ribbon will cross under the applique shape on the inside of the sweater. Weave the ribbon in the "X" pattern under all three appliques.

Figure 36-5: Ribbon weaving on all four sides of the argyle applique.

6 To secure the knots at the end of each line of weaving so they will not come undone, very carefully apply a tiny drop of Fray Check or other seam sealant on the knot. Place a piece of paper or scrap fabric under each knot before you treat it with seam sealant so that you won't drip any of the liquid onto the sweater.

7 On the wrong side of the sweater, fuse a small patch of interfacing over the point at which the ribbons cross under the argyle. This helps to keep the ribbons adjusted on the sweater front (Fig. 36-6).

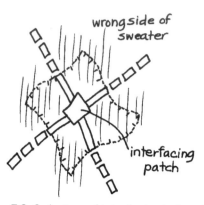

Figure 36-6: A piece of interfacing is fused over the intersecting ribbons on the back of the sweater to secure the ribbons to the garment.

The only thing this sweater needs is your designer label (see Section 41) and you're ready to wear it.

Bright Idea

Location, location, location—it's supposed to be the secret to success in business and real estate. But it's also the secret to success for any garment you trim. Where you choose to locate a design is crucial to the final effect. Take time to plan where the design will be placed on your T-shirt, sweater, or jacket. Try on the garment to test your plans and ideas. Your sewing time and talents are wasted if the decoration lands in a nonflattering area or gets wrinkled up in the garment folds when it is worn.

Tone-on-Tone Appliqued Sweater

37

I purchased a matching V-neck sweater and crinkled skirt, but the skirt was too long. To fix the length and to have fabric for the appliques on the sweater, I removed part of the *top* of the skirt rather than cutting from the bottom (Fig. 37-1). A crinkled skirt would be a real challenge to hem. Matching color (or tone-on-tone) appliques have proven to be a popular new direction in decorating garments. Though the effect is subtle and hard to see from a distance, the total look is classy and understated, like expensive ready-to-wear. See my sweater on page 125.

Figure 37-1: To obtain applique fabric to match the sweater and shorten the skirt at the same time, I cut off the top of the matching skirt and reattached the elastic waistband.

SUPPLY LIST

1 PULLOVER V-NECK SWEATER

¹⁄₄ YD. (23CM) PAPER-BACKED FUSIBLE WEB

FABRIC TO MATCH THE SWEATER

¹⁄₄ YD. (23CM) STABILIZER

1 Where can you find fabric to match your sweater? You have other options besides cutting the fabric from a matching skirt. Check the shoulder pads (if any), sometimes they're covered with fabric to match the sweater. Perhaps the pockets in a skirt or pair of pants can be removed or replaced, or maybe the matching wide fabric belt can be taken apart and used for tone-on-tone appliques (Fig. 37-2). Of course, you can also check your stash of fabrics as well as fabric stores.

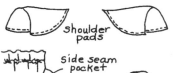
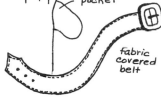

Figure 37-2: Sometimes you can find matching fabric on these parts of ready-to-wear clothing.

Tone-on-tone decorations are gaining in popularity because they are sophisticated and subtle. Self-fabric appliques can be created from a garment's fabric-covered shoulder pads, fabric-covered belt you don't plan to wear, hemline, or pockets. On this dress, one pocket was removed and used to create the 1" (2.5cm) fabric squares that were stitched to the dress front. The appliques are sewn with blue thread, to match the dress neck lining.

2 Select an applique design for the sweater or use the set of triangles in Figure 37-3. Trace the designs onto paper-backed fusible web, and fuse the web to the applique fabric. With the crinkled skirt fabric, I found that I could increase or decrease the wrinkled effect by flattening or pulling on the fabric. Cut out the designs and remove the paper backing. Now you can arrange the shapes on the sweater until you arrive at a pleasant layout. You can always pin the shapes to the sweater and try it on to check the location of the designs. Once your layout is finalized, fuse the shapes to the sweater.

3 Before sewing the designs, be sure to add stabilizer to the wrong side of the sweater beneath the fused-on appliques. Stabilizer is extremely important to use when sewing on sweaters, as the knits are generally loose and added fabric and stitching could cause distortion (Fig. 37-4). I have successfully used both tear-away and water-soluble varieties of stabilizer. If the sweater must be dry-cleaned, a water-soluble stabilizer might not be the best choice.

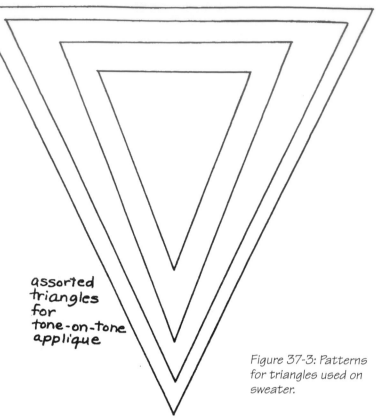

assorted triangles for tone-on-tone applique

Figure 37-3: Patterns for triangles used on sweater.

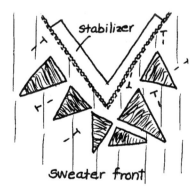

Figure 37-4: Add stabilizer to the sweater before stitching the appliques.

4 Now it's time to choose your stitching style. Traditional satin stitching is one choice, but your sewing machine probably offers many other selections. For my sweater, I chose a feather stitch and light gold thread so that the stitching would be slightly visible on the edges of the triangles. Select your thread color based on how visible you want the stitching to be. In many sweater knits, stitches that extend past the edges of the applique shapes sink into the knit and are not very noticeable. I suggest experimenting with thread colors and stitches on scraps of the applique fabric. Once you begin to sew directly on the sweater, you may find that the stitches look different because of the depth and stretch of the knit. Begin sewing and check the work after a short distance. If you don't like it, you won't have too many stitches to remove before you start sewing again. Pick a decorative stitch and sew around the edges of the appliques.

5 After the stitching is complete, remove the stabilizer from the back of the sweater. Do this with care. Instead of vigorously ripping away the stabilizer, hold your thumb over part of the stitching and tear away from that section of sewing. This way, the stitching and the knit fabric are protected from distortion.

There's a difference of opinion about the sweater shown on the next page. My friend Nancy says it needs some gold or green beads, and my sister Sarah says it looks good as it is. You can decide what you think. Add all the appliques and extra details you feel your sweater needs to give it your particular brand of style.

Tone-on-Tone Appliqued Sweater
Pieces of fabric cut from the skirt of this matching outfit were used for the sweater appliques.

In this close-up view of the tone-on-tone applique, the subtle details of the crinkled fabric and the decorative stitching attaching the fabric triangles are visible.

Dress with Ribbing Applique

38

Does this sound familiar? The dress fits, the color is great, and it would be wonderful to wear if the neck ribbing weren't so tight, binding like a rubber band around your neck (Fig. 38-1). That's exactly how I felt about the dress shown in the photo—until I realized that the ribbing could be removed and used to create an applique. The dress now has a comfortable circular neckline and some unique appliques.

Figure 38-1: A too-tight ribbed neck makes any dress uncomfortable to wear.

SUPPLY LIST

1 DRESS OR TOP WITH TURTLENECK (OR MOCK TURTLENECK) RIBBING

TISSUE WRAPPING PAPER

1/2 YD. (46CM) FABRIC FOR NECKLINE FACING

1/4 YD. (23CM) LIGHTWEIGHT FUSIBLE INTERFACING (TRICOT KNIT)

1/4 YD. (23CM) STABILIZER

1/4 YD. (23CM) PAPER-BACKED FUSIBLE WEB

1   Before cutting the neck ribbing off the dress, it's a good idea to staystitch the neckline. Straight stitch on the wrong side of the dress, sewing very close to the neck seam line, possibly moving the needle to the right needle position (Fig. 38-2).

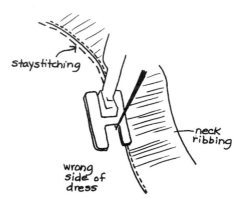

Figure 38-2: Staystitch around the dress neckline before cutting off ribbing.

2   Carefully cut the ribbing from the dress. Press the new dress neckline and fold it in half, meeting the two shoulder seams and forming folds at the center front and center back of the dress. Lay the folded neckline curve on a piece of tissue paper (Fig. 38-3). To make the facing pattern, trace the line from the front fold line along the neckline curve and up to the center back fold. Make the facing 2" (5cm) wide. To duplicate ready-to-wear garment facings, you may prefer to cut the center back facing wider.

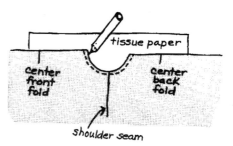

Figure 38-3: Fold the dress at the center front and back, and draw the neckline facing pattern.

Dress with Twisted Serger Strips and Dress with Ribbing Appliques

Long fabric strips (fabrics by VIP) with serged edges are twisted and sewn to the blue dress for an elegant look (Section 39). On the teal dress, a subtle accent is created by cutting an applique design from the neck ribbing band of the dress, which was removed because it was too tight. Yarn is stitched to outline the design (Section 38).

3 Place the facing pattern on a folded piece of facing fabric as shown in Figure 38-4, and cut out a fabric facing. Use the same technique to cut a facing from the interfacing.

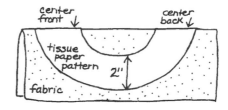

Figure 38-4: The new neckline facing pattern is 2" (5cm) wide.

Fuse the interfacing to the wrong side of the facing fabric and either trim the outer edge of the facing with pinking shears, or serge or zigzag this edge. Place, pin, and sew the right side of the facing to the right side of the dress neckline, matching center front and back points (Fig. 38-5).

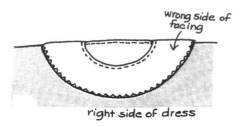

Figure 38-5: Sew the facing to the dress neckline.

Trim and clip into the seam allowance. Press and understitch by sewing the seam allowance to the facing, as shown in Figure 38-6.

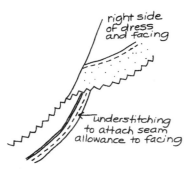

Figure 38-6: Stitching the seam allowance to the facing helps to keep the facing from showing on the right side of the dress.

Secure the facing to the dress by topstitching from the right side of the garment (Fig. 38-7). Now you're ready to trim the dress with a ribbing fabric applique.

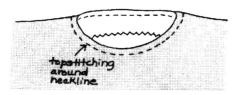

Figure 38-7: Topstitching secures the facing to the inside of the dress neckline.

4   If there is a seam in the ribbing, cut the ribbing at the seam line to create a flat piece of fabric rather than a circular tube. Press the ribbing thoroughly, using a water spray and steam. If there is a noticeable fold line that is difficult to press out, try applying some white vinegar to the fold and pressing again. This age-old remedy has removed many hemline marks and firmly pressed fold lines.

5   Select an applique design to cut from the ribbing. The dimensions of the ribbing will limit your selection. I used the design shown in Figure 38-8 and cut the two small separate pieces of the design from the neckline facing fabric. To recreate my design, trace the designs in Figure 38-8 onto paper-backed fusible web, fuse the web to the wrong side of the ribbing and facing fabrics, and cut out the design shapes. Peel off the paper and arrange the shapes on the garment to create an attractive design. You will notice that the design on my dress is placed to the side of the neckline rather than centered on the front (Fig. 38-9).

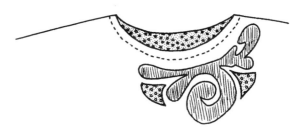

Figure 38-9: The appliques were set slightly off-center.

Experiment with design positions to see what is more pleasing to your eye. Pin the shapes to the dress and try it on to make sure the design will look good when the garment is worn. Once you've finalized your design layout, fuse the shapes to the front of the dress.

6   With stabilizer on the wrong side of the dress front, sew the designs to the garment. I used a thread that was slightly lighter than the dress and attached the appliques with a blanket stitch. Afterward, I couched yarn around the large design (see "What is Couching" on p. 56).

The design and the ribbing fabric are a subtle addition to the dress, a tone-on-tone look that is easy to create with the ribbing fabric taken right from the dress. This dress is sure to get compliments on its interesting textured design. And you won't have a headache from a too-tight neck ribbing.

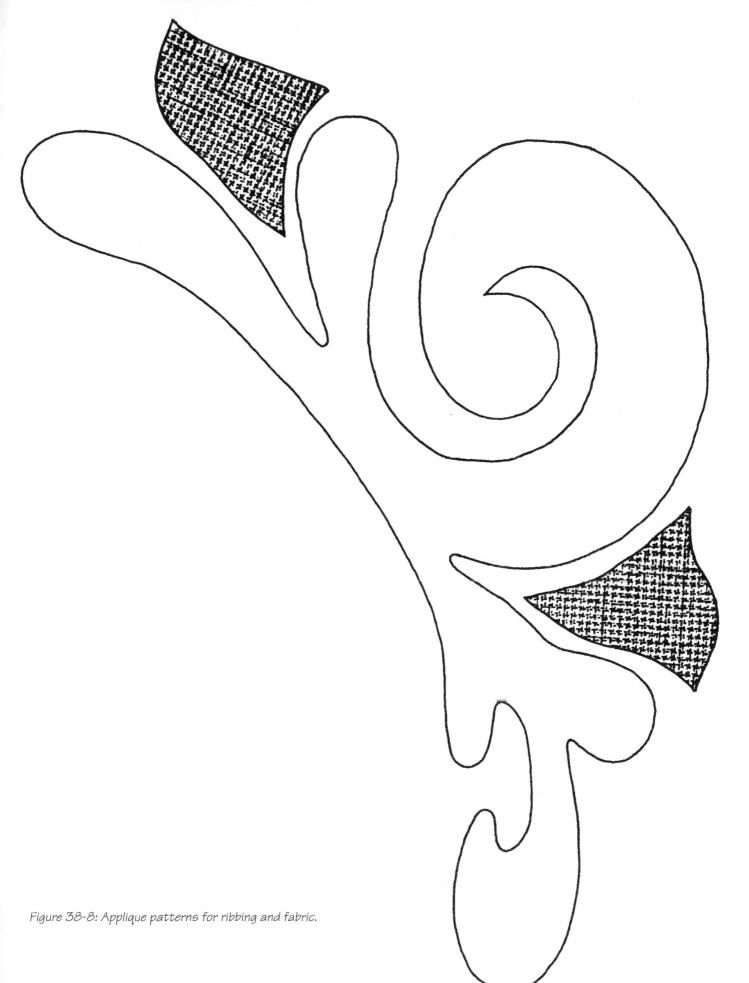

Figure 38-8: Applique patterns for ribbing and fabric.

Dress with Twisted Serger Strips

39

SUPPLY LIST

1 DRESS WITH A PLAIN FRONT

1 YD. (0.95M) EACH OF TWO FABRICS FOR DECORATIVE STRIPS

¾ YD. (68.5CM) STABILIZER (OPTIONAL)

*L*ong, reversible fabric strips with serged edges are twisted and sewn to a dress front for dimensional trim (Fig. 39-1). Select soft cotton fabrics for this project to avoid too much bulk at the twisted areas of the strips.

1 The first step of this project is the preparation of the serged strips of fabric. As you'll notice on the dress in the photo, the strips are of different widths; I used 1″ (2.5cm), 1½″ (4cm), and 1¾″ (4.5cm) strips and suggest that anything wider than 1¾″ is difficult to twist and creates a too-thick lump at the twist point. You'll make five 1-yd. (0.95m) strips altogether.

2 Lay out the fabrics with wrong sides together. You can premark the widths of the strips or you can use a marking on the serger to guide you. Set the serger to stitch a standard four-thread stitch, or a narrower three-thread rolled edge. I used a rolled hem and chose Woolly Nylon thread for the upper looper with a color that matched the Woolly Nylon for the standard thread in the lower looper. Hold the two fabrics together and serge strips off in the widths you've determined. Robbie Fanning suggests spray starching if you have trouble holding the fabrics together. After one edge is serged, serge off another strip. Go back to serge-finish the second edge of each strip (Fig. 39-2).

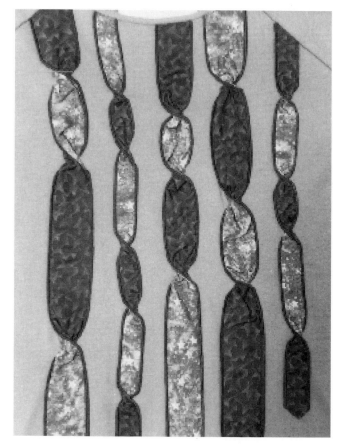

Figure 39-1: Serge together layered fabric strips and then twist them before sewing them to the dress. It's a fun, easy technique that adds style to a dress front.

Figure 39-2: With the wrong sides of the two fabrics together, serge off strips.

3 For an accurate placement of the serged strips, draw lines on the dress front. Each twisted strip will be aligned on the lines you've drawn. Turn under and pin the raw edges at the top of each strip to meet the dress neckline. Pin a portion of the strip to the dress, then make a twist in the strip, pinning the twist to the dress (Fig. 39-3).

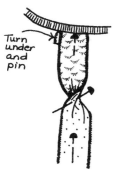

Figure 39-3: Turn under and pin the top edges of the strips; pin the strips and twists in place.

Now the reverse side of the strip will show. Pin down the strip with the second fabric showing, and then twist the strip again. Do this for a total of three to five twists per strip. At the bottom of the strip, fold the edges into a point, as shown in Figure 39-4, or turn under the edge for a straight or tapered look. Finish positioning, pinning, and twisting each strip. Use plenty of pins. You'll be glad you did when you take the dress to the sewing machine to sew the strips in place.

Figure 39-4: Ways to fold under the bottom edges of the serger strips.

4 Use a straight stitch to sew along all of the edges of the strips; begin at the neck edge (Fig. 39-5). All of the pins you used will hold the fabrics together accurately. I also used an awl as I guided the sewing machine needle around the twisted areas. (I have only recently begun to use an awl, and have really appreciated how well it guides fabric toward the needle. Am I the last one to catch on to this wonderful basic tool?)

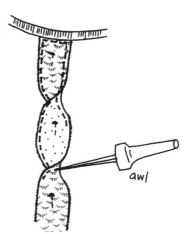

Figure 39-5: Sew down both sides of the twisted strips. An awl can help you guide the stitching.

5 Sew one strip to the dress and check the results before sewing further. A stabilizer on the back of the dress fabric is not usually necessary, but if the sewing puckers the dress too much, you may need to add it.

6 After all the strips are sewn in place, press the dress from the wrong side first, then press on the top side.

You could sew the twisted strips onto the dress in curving lines rather than straight ones. For a different effect, simply fold the strips instead of twisting them (Fig. 39-6).

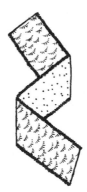

Figure 39-6: Try folding the serged strips instead of twisting them.

Aprons
Part Eight

Three Trim Ideas for Butcher-Style Aprons

40

Clearly an intelligent choice for covering your clothing as you work in the kitchen, the bib or butcher style apron is a favorite. Though they're easy to sew, they're even easier to buy and they're available at restaurant-supply, craft, and sewing stores. See my decorated versions on the next page.

My recommendation is that you buy a supply of these basic aprons to decorate for gifts and special occasions. White aprons are the easiest ones to find, and they generally are less costly than colored aprons. I suggest you launder the aprons before trimming them; they usually have a lot of sizing in the fabric, making them stiff. Here are three ways to improve and decorate them.

Kitchen-Print Apron

SUPPLY LIST

1 PLAIN BUTCHER-STYLE APRON

3" (7.5CM) PIECE OF VELCRO

1/4 YD. (23CM) KITCHEN-PRINT FABRIC (OR ENOUGH TO SHOW ONE REPEAT OF THE DESIGN IN THE PRINT)

1 I first cut the neck strap at the center back of the apron and added a Velcro closure. The neck straps are usually very long on these aprons, and the Velcro closure makes it easier to put the apron on and adjust the neck opening for people of all sizes.

2 I also changed the length of this apron. I cut 8" (20.5cm) from the bottom of the apron and resewed the piece to the new bottom edge of the apron. I then sewed a row of pockets into the piece. This feature gives a useful addition to the apron (Fig. 40-1).

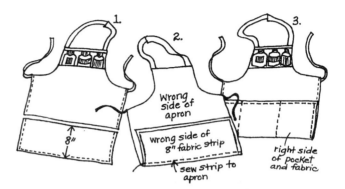

Figure 40-1: Cut off and reattach the bottom 8" (20.5cm) of the apron to make a row of pockets.

3 The trim across the top of the apron is typical of the attractive kitchen prints available in fabric stores. For a friend who enjoys canning and making pickles, this print is a perfect choice. Simply cut a section of the fabric, turn under the edges, and sew it to the apron.

This apron makes a wonderful gift, and it won't take you long to add the decorations and improvements.

Coffee Break Apron

The burgundy apron in the photo features an applique appropriate for many coffee and tea enthusiasts. The apron came with the adjustable buckle on the side of the neck strap, a detail that you could add to any apron.

SUPPLY LIST

1 PLAIN BUTCHER-STYLE APRON

TRACING PAPER

COTTON SCRAPS FOR APPLIQUE

1/4 YD. (23CM) TEAR-AWAY STABILIZER

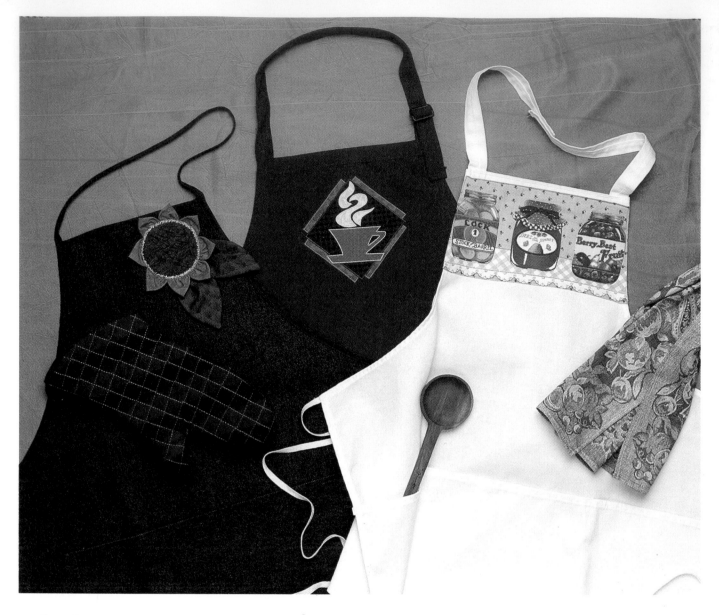

Three Trim Ideas for Butcher-Style Aprons

A dimensional sunflower trims the denim apron by Bagworks at left. On the center maroon apron from Alpha Shirt Company, a coffee cup applique enhances the plain apron. A kitchen-print border fabric from Concord gives color to the white butcher apron; a row of pockets is created by cutting off and reattaching the bottom 8" (20.5cm) of the original apron.

1 This is a simple machine applique project. Trace the design in Figure 40-2 onto paper-backed fusible web. Cut apart the pieces of the design and fuse them onto the fabrics you're using for the project. Cut the shapes out of the fabric, remove the paper backing from them, and arrange them on the apron front.

2 When you're satisfied with the arrangement of the shapes, fuse them into place on the apron. Using a stabilizer behind the apron, stitch the shapes to the apron with a satin stitch, remembering to stitch the bottom layer of the image first.

Sunflower Apron

The third apron is made of denim, a good color and durable fabric for a task apron. It's a good choice for the garden as well as the kitchen. Or maybe, like my sister Ruthie, you appreciate an apron with pockets to wear while you're sewing or quilting. She thinks it's a habit every sewing enthusiast should develop. The sunflowers trimming the apron add cheerful trim and a dimensional design.

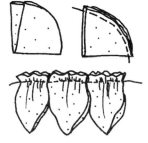

Figure 40-2: Coffee Break applique pattern.

SUPPLY LIST

1 DENIM BUTCHER-STYLE APRON

1/4 YD. (23CM) FABRIC FOR PETALS

FABRIC SCRAPS FOR FLOWER CENTER AND LEAVES

1 From gold fabric, cut eight 3″ (7.5cm) circles for the petals using the pattern in Figure 40-3. Fold each petal into quarters and gather the cut edges 1/8″ (3mm) from the edge, stitching from one petal to another (Fig. 40-4).

Figure 40-4: Fold, stitch, and gather the flower petals into a circle.

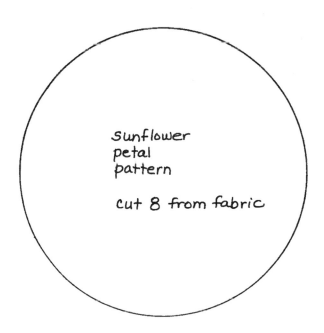

sunflower
petal
pattern

cut 8 from fabric

Figure 40-3: Circle pattern for sunflower petals.

Draw a 3″ (7.5cm) circle on the apron where you want the sunflower to be located. Pin and baste the petals around the circle, making sure that the gathering line is inside the circle (Fig. 40-5).

Figure 40-5: Place the gathered flower petals in a circle with the gathered edges inside the circle drawn on the background fabric.

2 The center of the flower is brown fabric. Trace a 3″(7.5cm) circle (Figure 40-3) onto paper-backed fusible web and fuse it to the wrong side of brown fabric. Cut out, remove the paper, and fuse the circle over the petals on the apron. Sew around the circle with a satin stitch to cover the edges. Depending on the thickness of the apron fabric, you may need to use stabilizer on the wrong side of the apron.

3 Another option for the flower center is to pucker-stitch it before cutting out the circle. It's best to test this technique before sewing the actual flower. On a lightweight piece of test fabric, sew intersecting lines, using a long stitch and tightening the needle tension on your machine (Fig. 40-6).

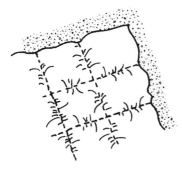

Figure 40-6: Pucker stitch the fabric for the flower center by adjusting the stitch length and tightening the needle tension.

Adjust the stitch length and needle tension until you like the look of the stitching, which will automatically gather the fabric. To increase the puckering, hold your index finger behind the presser foot and let the fabric bunch up after it is stitched. When you feel comfortable with the technique and are satisfied with the machine's settings, pucker-stitch a piece of fabric at least 5″ (12.5cm) in diameter

(or 2″ (5cm) larger than the final circle), which will become the flower center. You may want to fuse a piece of lightweight fusible interfacing to the wrong side of the puckered fabric to give it a little body. Then fuse on a circle of paper-backed fusible web to the wrong side of the puckered piece and cut the 3″ (7.5cm) circle from the treated fabric. Remove the paper backing and fuse and sew the circle over the edges of the petals as described in Step 2.

4 Use the leaf pattern in Figure 40-7 to make the large leaves. Cut out two leaves from fabric, place them right sides together, and sew around the two curved edges using a ¼″ (6mm) seam allowance. Turn the leaf right side out through the opening at the straight edge. Gather or tuck this straight edge and stitch it to the apron beneath the flower petals.

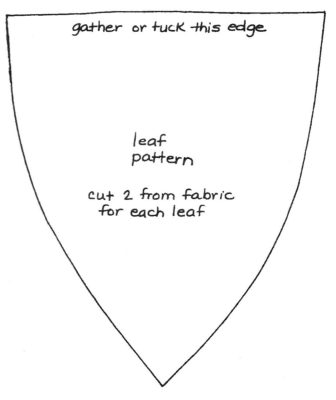

Figure 40-7: Leaf pattern.

Don't feel limited to sunflowers. You could use the petals, flower center, and leaf techniques to make pink or red or blue flowers—any color you want.

These apron suggestions are just the beginning of possibilities for you. The simple trimming ideas will be easy to complete in a short time. Often that's the kind of project we need to fit into our busy days and lives.

TRIM BY
SUSAN R.
STEVENSON
1995

An Original
by
Susan Kasten

sewing
Details
by
Rachel E. Koski
6-18-95

The Final
Addition
Part Nine

Designer Labels

41

Most painters and artists never complete a work of art without adding their name and perhaps the year to the margins of their work. Some of these names are prominent on paintings and add to the value and prestige of the artwork.

It's time for sew-ers to label their works of art. For us, the medium is fabric and thread rather than oil paint, watercolors, or clay. The final touch on all of the projects we complete should be a label with our name on it.

In this chapter I present a variety of ways to label the garments you have renovated with sewing techniques. You can replace the manufacturer's label in the garment or add to it. I hope some of my suggestions might work for you, and that I can encourage you to sign your sewing artwork, all of which is special and unique.

The easiest way to label garments is to purchase and use fabric labels specially designed for sewing into handmade clothing. If you have some of these labels now, be sure to use them on everything you stitch. Order them to give as gifts for other stitchers you know. Let's spread this good habit of labeling our work. If you don't have labels with your name on them, see "Supply Resources" on page 143. Many styles of woven and printed labels are available by mail order.

Besides straight stitching printed labels in place in the usual way, you can incorporate the labels into a more artistic application. Fuse paper-backed fusible web to the wrong side of the name label (some labels are already fusible). Fuse the label in place at the center back of the garment; then, over the cut edges of the labels, fuse small appliques

that tie in with the designs featured on the garment (Fig. 41-1). (On second thought, who says the labels have to be sewn to the center back neckline of the garment? That's the usual place we see labels, but maybe you'll find a better location for your name.)

Figure 41-1: Designer label with appliques covering the ends.

Add a fabric frame to your label by fusing or stitching it over a piece of decorative fabric (Fig. 41-2).

Figure 41-2: Framed designer label on decorative fabric.

Consider using the lettering capability of your sewing machine to stitch a label. Stitch on a plain piece of fabric, or a solid color area of a printed fabric. Fuse paper-backed fusible web to the wrong side of the fabric and leave the paper on. The paper serves as a stabilizer while you stitch and then when you're done sewing, the paper is removed and the label is ready for fusing. Draw a straight line on the fabric to help you guide the stitching. I recommend that you practice to get the feel of the spacing and stitching. After you've achieved lettering that meets your neatness standards, cut the edges of the fabric with pinking shears. Then peel off the paper. Voilà! It's a name label to fuse to a garment you've trimmed (Fig. 41-3).

Here are some of the possibilities for personalized designer labels. Make sure to add this final touch to any garment you trim.

Figure 41-3: Use sewing machine lettering to make your own distinctive labels.

Use machine lettering for another kind of label to add to the brand label already in the garment. In this way credit is given to the garment maker and to the garment transformer—you. Stitch "And (your name)" to a piece of fabric, as described above, or stitch your name onto a piece of ribbon with stabilizer behind it. Once again, practice sewing first. When you've stitched your name satisfactorily on the ribbon, tear away the stabilizer and sew your name tag at the bottom edge of the manufacturer's tag in the garment.

Sew strips of fabric to either a ready-made label or one you made yourself to frame the sewing artist's signature. The edges of the fabric strips will be turned under and pressed. Instead of sewing the enlarged label to the back of the garment neck in a straight position, sew it on at an angle. This will add a decorative touch to the inside of the garment (Fig. 41-4).

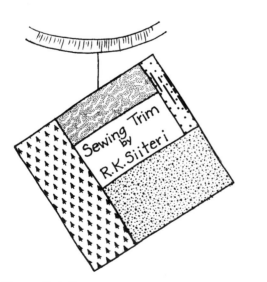

Figure 41-4: Frame a signature label with extra fabrics and place the label on an angle, just for fun.

Select a light, solid color fabric and make your own labels in your handwriting, or use the sample labels in Figure 41-5. Trace the labels from the book onto paper with a dark pen and then tape the label fabric securely to the paper. If you need help seeing through the fabric to the label pattern, tape both the paper and the fabric to a window. For a permanent label that will last through laundering, use a Sulky Iron-on Transfer Pen, a laundry pen, or other fine point permanent marker. Do some test writing with the pen before you do the label. This type of label can also be enhanced with decorative stitching or extra fabric.

Figure 41-5: Patterns for designer labels. Trace these from the book and add your name and the date.

Here's another label idea: Brush fabric paint on the back of a rubber stamp and press the stamp onto the label fabric. Using a permanent-ink pen, write your name and the year your creation was completed. Once the paint dries, after twelve hours, heat-set the stamping by ironing it (Fig. 41-6).

Figure 41-6: Designer label made with a rubber stamp and permanent-ink marking pen.

Where you sew the label can become a creative decoration. Because many ready-to-wear brands add their logos and labels on the outside of the garment, we can consider a similar application. There's nothing wrong with sewing your label to the front, side, or back—wherever you'd like to place your signature.

If you flip back through the photos in this book, you'll notice that I added a variety of labels to many of the projects shown. Enjoy combining the suggestions I've presented here and in those photos to create your own special labels. The people who receive your stitch-enhanced gifts or who purchase your stitching creations will be happy to find your signature on the label.

Bright Idea

Retail clothing stores are a great place to see the latest fashions and ideas we can duplicate thanks to our sewing skills. But let's not misbehave as we study the garments and racks of clothing. To boldly exclaim, "I don't have to buy that. I can easily make it" is not appropriate behavior. Consider the shop owner or buyer who spends hours selecting current, fashionable garments, hoping to please her customers and sell the clothing. She is not in business to provide us with ideas. So let's be discreet as we look at ready-to-wear. Take notes after you leave the store. Refrain from exclaiming over expensive prices and how you could make it yourself for mere pennies. When you find a garment that is just your style and has wonderful sewing ideas on it, buy it, wear it, and enjoy it. Even Julia Child eats in restaurants.

Bibliography

Bawden, Juliet. *The Art and Craft of Applique.* New York: Grove Weidenfeld, 1991.

Brown, Gail, and Young, Tammy. *Innovative Sewing.* Radnor, Pa.: Chilton Book Company, 1990.

Brown, Pauline. *Applique.* London: Merehurst Press,1990.

Hargrave, Harriet. *Mastering Machine Applique.* Lafayette, Calif.: C & T Publishing, 1991.

Mulari, Mary. *Accents for Your Style.* Aurora, Minn.: Mary's Productions, 1990.

Mulari, Mary. *Sweatshirts with Style.* Radnor, Pa.: Chilton Book Company, 1993.

Ward, Nancy. *Stamping Made Easy.* Radnor, Pa.: Chilton Book Company, 1994.

Supply Resources for Garments, Yarn, Labels, & Ultrasuede

Blank Garments & Accessories

Alpha Shirt Company
401 East Hunting Park Avenue
Philadelphia, PA 19124
(800-523-4585)
Full selection of T-shirts, sweatshirts, fashion, and active wear; free catalog.

Bagworks
3933 California Parkway E
Fort Worth, TX 76119
(817-536-3892)
Plain garments, fabric bags, and accessories; free catalog.

Max c.b.
255 West Broadway
Paterson, NJ 07522
(201-595-8001)
White 100% cotton fashion-forward garments; free catalog.

Sunbelt Sportswear
P.O. Box 791967
San Antonio, TX 78279
(210-349-3835)
Sportswear and accessories; full range of sizes from children's to women's plus; free catalog.

Yarns

Ogier Trading Company
P.O. Box 686
Moss Beach, CA 94038
Unique and interesting yarns; send a SASE for current brochure.

Threadline
P.O. Box 24925
Lexington, KY 40524
Write to request a current catalog and price list for designer threads.

Garment Labels

Blond Woven Label Company
20735 Darnestown Road, Box 26
Dickerson, MD 20842
(301-428-8334)
Free information.

Fabric Label Company of KDI
7746 Arjons Drive
San Diego, CA 92126
(619-566-4461)
Woven labels, hang tags, printed labels; $1 for information.

Heirloom Woven Labels
Box 428
Moorestown, NJ 08057
(609-722-1618)
Woven labels from England; small quantities available; free information.

Ident-ify Label Corporation
P.O. Box 140204
Brooklyn, NY 11214-0002
Send a SASE for information.

Namemaker
P.O. Box 43821
Atlanta, GA 30378
(800-241-2890)
Free information.

Northwest Tag & Label
110 Foothills Road
Lake Oswego, OR 97034
(503-636-6456)
$1 for information package.

Sterling Name Tape Company
P.O. Box 939
Winsted, CT 06098
(203-379-5142)
Low minimums on printed labels; $1 for information.

Ultrasuede in Small Pieces & Scraps

Michiko's Creations
P.O. Box 4313-M
Napa, CA 94558
Send a SASE for current information.

Ultramouse Ltd.
3433 Bennington Court—M
Bloomfield Hills, MI 48301
$2 for catalog.

Index

About Mary Mulari

*G*arments with Style is the latest in the series of sewing books by author and teacher Mary Mulari. As in all of her books, Mary gives concise, sew-er-friendly directions on how to embellish garments.

Taking inspiration from her travels, nature, architecture, and fashion, Mary brings her ideas to her workshop located in the north woods of Minnesota, where she develops her designs and techniques. Eye-catching designs, combined with her sense of what's new in fashion, have made her a success in the sewing world. In addition to writing books, Mary teaches seminars across the United States and Canada, tests new products for the sewing industry, and develops patterns for commercial pattern companies.

Mary's first book, *Designer Sweatshirts*, published in 1983, evolved from seeing a decorated sweatshirt at a craft show and having a desire to share her ideas on how to transform this comfortable garment into a fashion statement. New fashion trends and sewing techniques, along with increased interest in Mary's work, led Mary to write other books on similar topics. *Applique Design Collection, Country Style Appliques, Adventure in Applique, Accents for Your Style, Designer Wearables and Gifts, Deluxe Designs, Sweatshirts with Style,* and *Travel Gear and Gifts to Make* followed in rapid response to sew-ers' pleas for more designs and inspiration.

Mary's designs and writing have appeared in many publications, including *Woman's World, Workbasket,* and *Sewing Update Newsletter.* She has made several appearances on the television series *Sewing with Nancy* and was a guest on the public television show *The Art of Sewing with Sue Hausmann.*

Mary obtained a teaching degree in English from the University of Minnesota, Duluth, and taught junior high English before combining her skill of writing with her love of sewing. She and her husband, Barry, operate a retail store in Aurora, Minnesota. In addition to being a part of the business community, they are also involved in many community and volunteer activities.

Many readers have said that using the patterns and ideas in Mary's books is just like having her alongside of them in their sewing room; they feel as if they have found a friend. After meeting Mary through her books or seminars, you, too, will feel that Mary is your friend and sewing partner.

Mary Mulari welcomes questions, comments, and ideas from her readers. Write to her at: Box 87–C2, Aurora, MN 55705.

Sketch your own designer details on these blank garments.